The Tenement Saga

The Tenement Saga

The Lower East Side and Early Jewish American Writers

Sanford Sternlicht

THE UNIVERSITY OF WISCONSIN PRESS
TERRACE BOOKS

The University of Wisconsin Press
1930 Monroe Street
Madison, Wisconsin 53711

www.wisc.edu/wisconsinpress/

3 Henrietta Street
London WC2E 8LU, England

1   3   5   4   2

Printed in the United States of America

Library of Congress Cataloging-in-Publication Data
Sternlicht, Sanford V.
The tenement saga : the Lower East Side and early Jewish American writers /
Sanford Sternlicht.
p.   cm.
Includes bibliographical references and index.
ISBN 0-299-20480-4 (alk. paper)
ISBN 0-299-20484-7 (pbk.: alk. paper)
1. American literature—Jewish authors—History and criticism.
2. American literature—New York (State)—New York—History and criticism.
3. Authors, American—Homes and haunts—New York (State)—New York.
4. Jewish authors—Homes and haunts—New York (State)—New York.
5. Jews—New York (State)—New York—Intellectual life.
6. Judaism and literature—New York (State)—New York.
7. Lower East Side (New York, N.Y.)—Intellectual life.
8. Lower East Side (New York, N.Y.)—In literature.
9. Tenement houses—New York (State)—New York.
10. Lower East Side (New York, N.Y.)—History.
11. Immigrants in literature.   12. Jews in literature.   I. Title.
PS153.J4S74   2004
810.9′892407471—dc22   2004012828

Terrace Books, a division of the University of Wisconsin Press, takes its name
from the Memorial Union Terrace, located at the University of Wisconsin–Madison.
Since its inception in 1907, the Wisconsin Union has provided a venue for students,
faculty, staff, and alumni to debate art, music, politics, and the issues of the day.
It is a place where theater, music, drama, dance, outdoor activities, and
major speakers are made available to the campus and the community.
To learn more about the Union, visit www.union.wisc.edu.

This book is dedicated to the memory of my mother,
SYLVIA HILSENROTH STERNLICHT
(b. London, Eng., 1903; d. Bronx, N.Y., 1980),
and my father,
IRVING STANLEY STERNLICHT
(b. Tarnov, Galicia [Austrian Poland], 1898; d. Bronx, N.Y., 1978).

Contents

Contents

Preface

The story of the massive Jewish immigration to America from Eastern Europe (1882–1924) is one of the nation's greatest success stories. Fleeing racial and religious persecution, and seeking the political and economic freedoms available in the United States, these Jewish men, women, and children first settled on the Lower East Side of Manhattan, where they created a vibrant culture that had an enormous impact on the rest of the nation. That Lower East Side life and culture—especially the Jewish American writers who emerged from that culture—are the main subjects of this book.

This study is intended both as a literary and social history—a personal memoir of the author's childhood spent on the Lower East Side displayed through shards of memory, and a reference book that informs readers about the lives and works of the major Jewish American writers who emerged from what was then called the Jewish ghetto and who had a significant impact on American letters. In addition to the generalist, the intended audience for this book includes teachers and students of American literature and culture, Judaic studies, and urban historians.

With the end of World War II the Lower East Side of Manhattan, the birthplace of modern Jewish American identity, experienced an exodus of first- and second-generation American Jews. Today that process is nearly complete. Thus, this book has also been written for their grandchildren and great grandchildren, who may wish to know more about their ancestors' experiences in what has become the American Jewish homeland. Since roughly half of those women and men who are the children, grandchildren, or great-grandchildren of Jewish immigrants married gentiles, a few Yiddish words or a photo of a tenement street jammed with pushcarts may evoke thoughtful looks or perhaps even bring a tear to the eyes of their Jewish partner or parent.

This, then, is also a book about the "roots" mystique of the Lower East Side, perhaps the one site in the whole country where an American Jew may feel just a little less lonely. A part of that mystique and a product of place is the small but important group of Jewish American writers who emerged from the Lower East Side, that communal space of inchoate Jewish American culture. These writers wrote about their American homeland. Several made very significant contributions to American literature. Together they fashioned an immigrant saga. From the very beginning I have planned this book as an exercise in mnemonics and signification. My enterprise is to help you imagine a lost space within a past time, a space of continual change that was then and is now a space of hope.

By the early 1960s most of the Jewish immigrants and children of immigrants had left the Jewish ghetto. But this was also a time when "ethnic Americans" were seeking their "roots," whether in Africa, Ireland, Italy, Poland, Greece, Scotland, or even England. The age of genealogy had been born. For the descendants of Eastern European Jews now living in America, the birthplace of their ancestors, the lands those ancestors had lived in for five hundred years, was one vast graveyard. Where was their "homeland" to mythologize and sacralize? The only possibility was the Jewish ghetto of Old New York, the Lower East Side. The surviving commercial institutions and tenements became a tourist attraction and—dare I say—a historical theme park for American Jews.

The republication of a single book helped precipitate the revival of interest in—indeed, fascination with—the Lower East Side: Henry Roth's *Call It Sleep,* a partly autobiographical novel of life on the Lower East Side at the beginning of the twentieth century. First published in 1934 and forgotten during the Depression, the book was rediscovered by New York Jewish intellectuals in 1956, was reprinted in 1960, and was reissued in a mass-market paperback edition in 1964. From that time on *Call It Sleep,* an acknowledged masterpiece, became a primary cultural artifact of Jewish American history. Its contribution to the revisiting—and rewriting—of the Lower East Side Jewish experience is incalculable.

As a child living on the Lower East Side of Manhattan from the late 1930s through the early 1940s, I was immersed in a world that seemed grim, dirty, crowded, frightening, and dangerous. It was circumscribed by the East River to the south and east, Houston Street to the north, and Christie Street to the west. Beyond this square mile and a half or so I did not venture alone. Occasionally my parents took me to one of the Yiddish theaters on Second Avenue, between Houston and Fourteenth Streets.

In the sixth grade I realized that almost all the streets bore English names like Essex, Norfolk, Suffolk, Pitt, Broome, Houston, Stanton, Rivington, Forsythe, among others. Since almost everyone I knew was Jewish, I wondered why there were no streets named Cohen or Levy. A lesson in New York City history in junior high school revealed that the names belonged to early-eighteenth-century landowners and merchants or—in the case of Madison, Monroe, and Jefferson streets—early American presidents.

From my child's-eye perspective I never saw the skyscrapers of the financial district that now seem to loom over the Lower East Side. Of course, the World Trade Towers were not there then (or now, alas), but many other large buildings, like the Woolworth Building, surely were visible from open vistas such as Seward Park on East Broadway.

Chinatown and Little Italy were exotic lands that demarcated one border of my territory. Most of the people living in my "country" were Jews, some of whom were Orthodox—the bearded men wearing black suits and hats, the women mainly unseen. Most of the Jews of my Lower East Side were, like my parents, not very religious except on the High Holy Days. It was as if they had jettisoned much of their religion and their culture during the Atlantic crossing and had substituted nothing comparable.

Despite the preponderance of Jews living on the Lower East Side just before and during the early years of World War II, there were many gentiles living among them: African Americans, Chinese, Irish, Italians, Poles, and Ukrainians. Where were the "Americans"? We schoolchildren had no doubts. We were the Americans. Our teachers in the then excellent New York City public schools told us so. They taught us to be proud of American history. They instructed us in the correct usage of Standard American English. They provided the rudiments of mathematics, geography, and science. They showed us how to draw trains, ships, planes, and bridges in the Art Deco style. I remember the names of some of my teachers in Public School 31 and can still see their faces before me. Their work was supplemented by the Educational Alliance—the great East Broadway Settlement House—and by the mecca of all of who loved the transformative magic of books: the Seward Park Branch of the New York Public Library.

Of course we were indoctrinated. The great goal of the Lower East Side schools was Americanization. We were taught to believe in the American dream of social justice and equal opportunity for all people. Only much later were we to learn that it was just that, a dream, that most of us would never fully realize. Regardless of what an Old World rabbi or a socialist parent might have said, we bought it, and for some of us the dream came to pass. Furthermore, when the United States entered World War II, thousands of Lower East Side youths—like Uncle Charley and a dozen of my cousins—went off to war and battle wounds, never doubting that they were fighting for their own country. And when I was called upon to serve, I did so unbegrudgingly.

In the tenement flats my family inhabited, first on Madison Street and then on Henry Street at the corner of Jefferson, my father had one small bookcase containing about forty books in English. I tore through them as soon as I could read. Two left a profound impression on me as I approached my teen years: *The Rise of David Levinsky* by Abraham Cahan and *Jews Without Money* by Michael Gold. The latter title perplexed me, for I didn't know any Jews *with* money. Were there any? None I could see on the Lower East Side. Certainly not my widowed grandmother, who earned pennies plucking chickens, nor my laboring uncles, and certainly not my parents, with their tiny candy stand. The Cahan and Gold books were intriguing because they were about the people and places I felt I knew and understood. If people like my parents and the streets I roamed could be captured in books, then our world was recognized and it truly existed.

My father also had a partial set of Mark Twain's works that he had assembled, one volume a week, through a newspaper promotion. Well, *those* books—*Roughing It, Life on the Mississippi, The Mysterious Stranger*—were exotic to me.

The great appeal of the Lower East Side today is due to a number of facts. It is a place where poor people—mostly non-Jews—still live under difficult conditions. Oddly, though located in lower Manhattan and near the financial capital of the world, it has not been subject to gentrification, although that is beginning to change. It stands in contradistinction to the flatness and cultural vacuity of the American suburban landscape.

This book is, in part, an excursion into the changing landscape of my memory, an act of remembrance. For the first part I have culled my Lower East Side childhood recollections, fully realizing that I have not, after so many decades, remembered events perfectly. I hold on to versions of experiences concretized or diminished by time and altered in the process of thinking and telling. Alas, no relative who shared these experiences remains alive to correct or confirm what my mind knows. All have emigrated again, this time to the vast, lifeless, haunting fields of stone in Brooklyn, Queens, and Staten Island. I do believe, however, that my particular use of memory—the act of bearing witness—serves the present and perhaps even the future.

For American Jews the Lower East Side reminds us of a time when we were poor. In the first half of the twentieth century it was the only place in America where Jews lived in an organic community (like a huge shtetl) where they felt at home and at ease. Ultimately it represents a major part of the twentieth-century Jewish epic: exodus across the water from European persecution by those who dared; a rise to prosperity in the new promised land; horror and guilt for those who were left or remained behind in the old country when the Black Night and the Blood Red Sea closed over them. My talks to students visiting the Lower East Side prompt me to remind my sons in Boston and Los Angeles that when their father was a child, his parents were as poor as that African American or Hispanic woman who cleans their high-tech offices at night, and they should fold that fact into their politics.

Much of the physical world of my childhood still exists. Frequent tours crisscross the Lower East Side of Manhattan. Most of the Jews are gone, but the streets, which have always been the haven of immigrants, now have new Americans—Puerto Ricans, Chinese,

Afro-Caribbeans, and others—pursuing their dream. And I, too, have become a cicerone to the memory of the Jewish immigrants who sailed the Atlantic to what they called—sometimes in breathless wonder, at other times in bitter derision—the Golden Land.

Acknowledgments

Thanks to Professor Ken Frieden, Rudolph Professor of Judaic Studies at Syracuse University, and Professor Harvey Teres of the English Department of Syracuse University, for help with research. Thanks also to the Holstein Foundation for many years of support for my Judaic Studies course on the literature of early Jewish American writers working in English, their adopted language. From the beginning I have felt it a privilege to teach the course. The present book grew out of that course.

My thanks also to Wendy Bousfield of Syracuse University Library and its interlibrary loan department; Dr. Robert Mandel of the University of Wisconsin Press; research assistant Clarice Touwsma; and my patient partner and excellent editor Mary Beth Hinton.

Part One

The Lower East Side

Cultural History and Topography

Where Did They Come From?

In the eighteenth century Poland was "devoured" by its three giant neighbors: Russia, Austria, and Prussia. As a result, the Polish Jewish community, by far the largest in the world, was divided into three parts, the biggest of which came under the rule of the Russian Empire. Before and after the division, the Ashkenazi Jews of Poland considered themselves a single community with a common vernacular language: Yiddish (Jewish). Russia, the least enlightened of the three conquerors, inherited the largest number of Jews and was least comfortable with these new and different subjects. The Russian government immediately set about trying to contain the Jews in a restricted area called the Pale, and to isolate them from urban life and economic opportunity—without total success. The government simultaneously attempted to undermine Jewish religion and culture through Russification and long periods of military service for young Jewish men, few of whom survived the brutality and the diseases endemic to the Russian army.

On 1 March 1881 Czar Alexander II was assassinated by Russian revolutionaries determined to overthrow the despotic rule of the Romanov dynasty. The bomb throwers, some of whom were Jewish intellectuals, naively hoped that the assassination would lead to a general uprising of peasants and workers throughout the vast empire. Instead, diverted by government officials and the Russian Orthodox

Church, peasants and workers turned on the Jewish population in a series of pogroms. These murderous rampages set in motion an enormous European emigration. Jews from Russia (including Lithuania, the Ukraine, and Byelorussia) wishing to flee the persecution moved west, seeking the relative freedom offered by those countries that had experienced the Enlightenment and were thus more tolerant than Russia.

The Jewish populations of what was now Austria-Hungary and Rumania caught the emigration fever and joined the human river that was diverted to Hamburg and other Baltic ports in 1882 in order to get the refugees aboard ships that would take them out of continental Europe. The primary destinations were the United States, the United Kingdom of Great Britain and Ireland, and Canada. The river of people flowed until 1924, when the United States, now in a racist mode, essentially limited immigration to British, Irish, and German immigrants, a policy that continued until the revolutionary liberalization of immigration laws in the 1960s. From 1881 to 1924 1.5 million Jews (almost half of them children) left the shtetlach (villages) and cities of Eastern Europe. Almost all came to the United States, most winding up in New York City.

It should also be noted that from the 1890s to 1924 more than ten thousand Jews immigrated from Greece and from the faltering Ottoman Empire. Their worship was Sephardic (the Ladino-Spanish) tradition, not Ashkanazic (the Central and Eastern European German-Yiddish tradition). They spoke not Yiddish but rather Ladino-Spanish, Greek, Turkish, and/or Arabic.

During this period the overwhelming majority of Jewish emigrants who sailed to America settled on the Lower East Side of Manhattan among the children and grandchildren of earlier German and Irish immigrants. There were families as well as single men and women. Most were poor. Although the majority had useful skills—dressmaking, tailoring, sewing, baking, cooking, woodworking, butchering, metalworking, carpentry, painting, brewing, distilling, and retailing—obtaining fair wages often was contingent upon fluency in English and organized unions. Many had been successful as small-business owners. They were fluent in Yiddish and generally also spoke one or more of the other Eastern European

4

languages. The most religious were skilled in the biblical languages of Hebrew and Aramaic. All hoped to find acceptance and economic opportunity—if not for them then for their children. They arrived with several bundles of clothes, religious books, candlesticks, and a few household items.

An intriguing question remains: Why did the shtetl Jews take so well to the urban environment? Their descendants continue to remain concentrated in and around New York, Chicago, Los Angeles, Philadelphia, and Boston. The shtetl Jews generally were not peasant farmers in Eastern Europe, so there was little likelihood that they would seek agricultural opportunities in the New World. Their craft-related occupations, like tailoring or blacksmithing, plus their role as middlemen in the agricultural production-to-consumer chain fit in with urban life. The most significant factor, however, was the dawning realization that besides political and religious freedom, which were offered elsewhere in the United States, in a metropolis like New York City there was also the freedom of willed anonymity. In the shtetl the Jew was marked as such by clothing, language, and association. In New York a Jewish man could shave off his beard. A married Orthodox Jewish woman could discard her wig. They could buy some American-style clothes, walk out of the ghetto, and be looked upon and treated like any another person walking down the street. Coupled with fluency in English, the possible transformation was complete.

The first time I ventured out of the Lower East Side alone was at the age of eleven, when I saw a newspaper advertisement for Beard and Beard's 1942 edition of *The History of the World* on sale for two dollars at Gimbel's Department Store in Herald Square. I was intent on buying a brand-new book for the very first time, and this is the one I wanted. I boarded the subway at East Broadway, rode to Thirty-fourth Street, walked to Gimbel's, found the book department, and bought the book. On the way to Gimbel's I wandered through the shopping crowd. I suddenly felt very mature and liberated. I was not a Lower East Side Jewish kid straying from his appointed place but rather just another American going shopping. I found that I actually had some control over my identity. Anonymity was delightful. At that moment I felt so free that I remember it vividly as I write. It was really wonderful not to be on the defensive, to be no one in particular for the first time.

Jews have lived in New York City since the mid-seventeenth century. The first Jews to land in New York City arrived in 1654, refugees from persecution in Recife, Brazil, where the Portuguese and the Inquisition had recently taken over from the Dutch. These twenty-three Sephardic Jews were members of the Dutch West India Company headquartered in Amsterdam. The ship carrying them to a place of refuge was seized on the high seas by Spanish pirates, who robbed and abandoned them on an island in the West Indies, where they were rescued by a French vessel sailing for Montreal. Considerately, the captain put the Dutch Jews ashore in Dutch New Amsterdam, but Peter Stuyvesant, the anti-Semitic last governor of New Amsterdam, confined them until the Amsterdam headquarters ordered their release. Help came to these destitute and forlorn people from Jewish communities in the West Indies, Holland, and London. The latter contact proved most propitious. After England seized New Amsterdam in 1664 during a war with Holland, the Jews of New Amsterdam thrived in the British colony of New York. Their numbers were never great and, given the tolerant conditions of an English colony and the equally tolerant atmosphere of the State of New York in the post-Revolutionary period, many of the prosperous Jews were assimilated into the Christian community.

In the nineteenth century tens of thousand of Ashkenazi German Jews came to America before, during, and following the European revolts of 1848. They were part of an enormous German immigration to the United States. Gentile and Jew settled on the Lower East Side at the same time that a massive Irish immigration—the result of the great potato famine of 1845–49 and its aftermath—also arrived in New York City's Lower East Side.

The area where the German and German Jewish immigrants first established their homes and businesses—first from the Bowery east to Pitt Street and then above Delancey Street north to Fourteenth Street and from Second Avenue to the East River—was called *Kleindeutschland*. From this group of Jewish immigrants eventually emerged the successful uptown merchants, professionals, and financial leaders, who looked with horror upon the poor, hungry, and frightened Eastern European Jews who flooded into the tenements of the Lower East Side in the final decades of the nineteenth century. They seemed so different from the Western Jews they had always known and appeared to pose a threat as to how they, the "Old Family" German Jews, would be perceived by the gentile American community in New York City.

The tide of Jews increased in volume as Eastern European Jews came to understand that they were part of a massive movement of people like themselves. They realized that it was a special time and place. They believed that despite hardships they could successfully transplant at least some of their vibrant Jewish culture to a new world. They would have the freedom and opportunity to make of their lives—and their children's lives—what their abilities could achieve. In the very act of leaving home and sailing steerage across the Atlantic, their dreams began to materialize, and the anticipated process of betterment commenced.

The year 1910 saw the high tide of Jewish immigration to America. At that time the greater Lower East Side housed more than five hundred thousand people in two square miles. It was then that the Lower East Side came to be known as the Jewish ghetto. The adjoining communities of Little Italy and Chinatown were minuscule in comparison to the Jewish community. The expression "Lower East Side," signifying that ghetto, also came into use at the beginning of the twentieth century.

Throughout much of the nineteenth century immigrants had come ashore from the ships docking at the East River piers located at the southeastern end of Manhattan. They stepped into Manhattan's Tenth Ward, east of the Broadway dividing line between east and west. When, in 1855, Castle Garden (formerly Fort Clinton) at the Battery became the first U.S. immigration center, and (after 1892) when ferries from Ellis Island brought the new immigrants ashore at the Battery, the immigrants could still walk into the tenement community. The filthy, unsanitary, overcrowded streets and tenements, as well as the anti-Semitic remarks that greeted "greenhorn" Jews, often overwhelmed the new immigrants, especially parents of young children and the elderly.

Affluent and concerned German Jews helped their co-religionists with such establishments as Mount Sinai Hospital (originally called the Jews' Hospital), the Hebrew Orphan Society, the Hebrew Sheltering and Guardian Society, and the Clara de Hirsch Home for Working Girls. Almost all patients at Mount Sinai Hospital were treated free of charge.

The Hebrew Immigrant Aid and Sheltering Society, founded by Lower East Side Jews, successor to the Hebrew Emigrant Aid Society (1881–83), was of inestimable help to the new immigrants through the high immigration period from the turn of the twentieth century until the Great Depression. The society even stationed representatives on Ellis Island to mediate between officials and Yiddish-speaking newcomers.

Settlement houses were of great help to immigrants of all ages. The term originated in the Jewish ghetto of London's East End, where social workers "settled" in Toynbee Hall to be close to their clients. In that district, in a tenement on Whitechapel Road where my maternal grandparents were then residing, my mother was born in 1903.

The University Settlement, founded as the Neighborhood Guild by Protestant philanthropists in 1886, was the first settlement house in the United States. It was originally established on Forsyth Street. In 1891 it moved to the corner of Rivington and Eldrige Streets, near the magnificent Eldridge Street Synagogue. The College Settlement was founded in 1889 by women from Smith College.

Two settlement houses I knew well are still in operation. The Educational Alliance (named for the merger of several agencies, including the Young Men's Hebrew Association and the Downtown Hebrew Institute, founded in 1889) came into being in 1893 on East Broadway and Jefferson Street, one block from my tenement home on the corner of Henry and Jefferson Streets. In that fondly remembered institution I learned to play the recorder and other useful things for a Lower East Side boy. The Henry Street Settlement, founded by Lillian Wald in 1893 as the Nurses' Settlement, was where my mother found preschool care for my little sister while she helped my father at our candy stand.

In general, the settlement houses helped immigrants learn English and other skills. They provided health services. They taught cooking, household care, tending the sick, and sanitation. Some taught music, dance, and art, including American and Jewish culture. The Henry Street Settlement was the first to offer a much-needed visiting nurse service. Of course, settlement houses existed in other sections of New York City and, indeed, in many other cities. Jane Addams's Hull House in Chicago, founded in 1899, was the most famous and most successful settlement house outside the Lower East Side. It may have been modeled, in part, after the Henry Street Settlement, although Hull House did not begin with nursing service.

Lower East Side Jews also looked after their own. They had come from individual communities in Europe, and for a while they maintained connections with the Old World town or shtetl. They quickly found and established relations with "lanzmen" in New York. Shortly after arriving in New York, in the last decades of the nineteenth century, they began to form *lansmanshafts* (organizations of people from the same European community) in the city. The many and varied functions of a lansmanshaft included serving as burial societies. Orthodox Jews had to be prepared for burial, mourned, and buried in specific ways and places. They wanted to spend eternity with their co-religionists—preferably friends and neighbors—just as they would have if they had died in Europe. The lansmanshafts bought large plots in Jewish cemeteries in Queens, Brooklyn, and Staten Island, making graves available inexpensively or free to their members. A Jewish Lower East Side immigrant would go without food before letting his or her membership in a lansmanshaft lapse. A father bought plots for his wife, himself, and often for his children. Today my father, mother, brother, and sister lie side by side in their Staten Island graves, just as my father had planned in the year 1941. Around them are buried members (and their families) of a Lower East Side organization he had joined in the 1920s.

Sometimes the lansmanshafts were housed in synagogues. Sometimes they turned into fraternal lodges similar to the Knights of Columbus or the Elks. The lansmanschaft gave charity to the poor, provided clothes to the needy, aided widows and their children, opened shelters for the unemployed and homeless, maintained the services of doctors, and provided free religious education to Jewish children. They collaborated with other Jewish organizations to establish hospitals on the Lower East Side, such as the Jewish Maternity Hospital, which was founded in 1906. Prior to this Jewish mothers either delivered their children at home with midwives or at the New York Lying-In Hospital, where the food was not kosher and few if any staff members spoke Yiddish. The lansmanshafts were important in the establishment of the Hebrew Free Loan Society in 1892, from which immigrants could obtain small loans to help them get started in business with a pushcart, a newsstand, or a tiny streetfront store. Lastly, the lansmanshafts helped in the founding of Jewish old age homes.

It must be stressed that although Jewish immigrants in the period of the exodus from Eastern Europe received much help from their German American co-religionists, as well as from the New York City government, Christian charities, and New York City philanthropic organizations, to a large extent they proudly helped each other.

Immigrant Life

In the great Eastern European Jewish migration, which lasted from 1882 to 1924, immigrants poured into New York City, with the vast majority residing in Manhattan on the Lower East Side, in Harlem, or in the boroughs of Brooklyn and the Bronx for the remainder of their lives. The Lower East Side was always crowded. As the twentieth century began, Jewish immigrants—having crossed the Atlantic in steerage, endured the processing and the fear of rejection on Ellis Island, and been dropped on the tip of Manhattan in the shadow of a forest of unbelievably tall buildings—now walked into a veritable cauldron of people, a maze of streets strewn with human waste, horse manure, and offal from slaughtered animals. From early dawn to midnight life seemed to gush out of the suffocating flats and shops, resulting in an endless stream of shouting men, babbling women, and shrieking children. So many of these new arrivals had come from shtetlach or small towns; now, in the two-square-mile sea of five-, six-, and seven-story tenements, they had to locate relatives or countrymen, find housing, obtain work, and learn a new language. Amazed by the overcrowded streets, journalists of the time described the Lower East Side as having a population density greater than Bombay or Calcutta. Encoded in the description was the belief—shared by many other New Yorkers—that the Lower East Side endangered the health and the standard of living of the rest of New York City and perhaps even the country.

The incredible scene was, of course, most daunting to the immigrants and their children, many of whom wondered why they had shouldered the cost and made the effort to come to the New World in the first place. A very tiny percentage returned to Europe as soon as they could. For my widowed grandmother Anna in 1900 there was no turning back. She immediately found work, first as a maid and then as a cook, earning enough money to provide for the year-old child who would become my father and also to send for her two older sons. They had been living in Tarnov, in the province of Galicia (Austrian Poland), and were being cared for by relatives. I wonder what she lived on during the few years she was saving to enfold my uncles Louis and Abie in her arms once more.

Grandma Anna lived her entire American existence successively in two cold-water tenement flats: the first was on Pitt Street (where large numbers of Jews from Galicia lived) and the second (after her children had grown up) on Norfolk Street. An early childhood memory of mine involves walking with my father east on Delancey Street to the live-chicken market under the Williamsburg Bridge, turning north on Pitt Street, and seeing my grandmother peering down from her third-floor window. Married and widowed a second time, she raised five children. Anna worked almost her entire eighty years. Her last job was plucking and singeing chicken feathers off newly slaughtered birds for a few pennies apiece.

Photos of the period, including those by the documentary photographer Jacob Riis, indicate how impassable the market streets were. People and stands jammed the sidewalks, while pushcarts commandeered the roadway. It seemed as if no horse and wagon could make its way through. Of course, not all streets were market streets, and on the Sabbath as well as in the evening the stands and pushcarts would disappear and the stores beneath the tenements would close. Then, if the weather was tolerable, the streets belonged to the children and their ball games. In the winter the stairways, hallways, and stoops sheltered the flock of children the Lower East

Side tenements housed. At the curbsides older boys and homeless men built fires made of ubiquitous, broken-up wooden crates to warm their hands or roast potatoes.

From just before World War I through the 1950s nearly 25 percent of the 1880s tenement house stock was demolished to increase public access and usage. A parkway between Forsyth and Chrystie Streets was planned after a scheme for improved housing in the immediate neighborhood was scrapped due to municipal corruption. Instead, a recreational park was constructed with playgrounds and ball fields. At the same time, schools and libraries rose up. Most significant, with funds from organized labor or New York State financing the city began the vast construction of a ring of high-rise housing along the East River, from the Brooklyn Bridge to East Fourteenth Street. Of course, the high-rises provided much better housing for many Lower East Siders. Unfortunately these buildings, along with the Franklin D. Roosevelt Drive, effectively barred the residents of the Lower East Side from access to the waterfront.

As the twentieth century progressed, the Lower East Side became less crowded, especially after open-immigration policies ceased in 1924. In fact, attempts to relieve overpopulation on the Lower East Side began in earnest when acres of tenements were razed to construct the Delancey Street entrance to the new Williamsburg Bridge. The bridge itself, which opened in 1903 and was only the second to link Manhattan to Brooklyn, was designed to ease Lower East Side congestion. It was familiarly called the "Jews' Bridge" because it specifically served the ghetto. As soon as it opened hundreds of Lower East Side families moved to the less-populated Williamsburg section of Brooklyn because workers could either walk across the bridge or take a trolley to the Lower East Side, where their garment-industry jobs were located. In ten years Williamsburg became almost as congested as the Lower East Side.

The tallest structure in my Lower East Side enclave that I can remember was—and still is—the ten-story Jewish Daily Forward Building around the corner from the family newspaper and candy stand on Henry and Jefferson Streets. Erected in 1912, it is now a national historic landmark; sadly, it no longer houses the greatest Jewish newspaper in America. Today the Lower East Side seems nearly deserted except for Delancey Street. Much of the street life has moved up into the high-rise public and private housing, with central heating, air conditioning, and television keeping people off the streets.

The Forward Building is on East Broadway, one of the favorite streets of my childhood. My library, the Seward Park branch, is on the street, as is Seward Park and the Educational Alliance. A second Jewish newspaper, *Der Tog* (The Day), was also published on the street when I was a child. Other Yiddish-language newspapers were also published on East Broadway earlier in the century, which explains why it bore the sobriquet Publishers' Row.

West of the Forward Building lies Nathan Straus Square (formerly Rutgers Square until 1931), at the junction of East Broadway, Rutgers, Essex, and Canal Streets, which was long the site of mass demonstrations and labor rallies, as was Seward Park. East Broadway was called the "Athens of the Lower East Side," with intellectuals, writers, and artists congregating in its coffee shops and little dairy restaurants, such as the Garden Cafeteria, where the staff of the *Forward* would meet for heated discussions over glasses of hot tea or cups of coffee. Among the Jewish literary immortals who worked on the paper and who frequented the cafeteria were Abraham Cahan (founder of the *Forward*), Isaac Bashevis Singer, and his brother and fellow novelist Israel Joshua Singer. For me East Broadway's greatest moments were when my heroic Uncle Charley, wearing his army uniform and a brace that supported his arm (he was wounded while fighting the Japanese in New Guinea), walked me down the street and took me into one of the restaurants to meet his friends and treat me to something delicious.

I do not wish to make my life—or that of any child of immigrants growing up on the Lower East Side—sound like an idyllic one. It was an ugly, dirty, and dangerous place for children. Although I did not—indeed, I could not—articulate it, I instinctively felt that, except for my parents, no one gave a damn about another ghetto kid. I was just one more faceless poor kid among tens of thousands, another creature passing through a neighborhood that for over two hundred years had housed waves of immigrants—many fresh off the boat—who were destined to rest eternally in graves located in the outer boroughs.

The ghetto existence outside my door was brutal. Teenage boys and even grown men terrorized and robbed little boys. My hard-working and distracted father seemed indifferent to or unaware of the terrors in my young life. More likely, he just didn't want to know about my troubles since he had plenty of his own, trying to keep his family fed and housed. I knew that my mother's repeated, facile advice—never fight; just run away; tell the teacher—was cowardly and wrong, weakening my resolve. I fought back and was beaten—but not always. I joined with other kids my age and we looked out for each other. Mother's advice might have made sense in Europe, where Jews were less than second-class citizens and were often fair game for robbery and rape, but I was an American kid. I made friends I could rely on to help me resist and not run from the fight. Like Sara Smolinsky in *Bread Givers,* one of Anzia Yezierska's autobiographical heroines, I realized that I alone had the responsibility to "make myself a person."

The Immigrant Woman and the Family

Although married Jewish immigrant women often accompanied their husbands to America and brought their children along too, sometimes they remained behind in Europe while he earned enough money to bring his family to New York. This was the only time she was not subject to continued pregnancies, for the immigrant mother very often had more children than she could reasonably handle. When sent for by her husband, the immigrant mother was responsible for bringing the European-born young by train to the German embarkation ports in the north, finding a ship, and caring for the children in the congested steerage holds while the vessel crossed the Atlantic.

Once settled on the Lower East Side, the immigrant mother's duties were many and exhausting. Besides taking care of her children and bearing more, there was cooking (which could include serving boarders as a function of administering to family business matters), cleaning, washing clothes by hand, and caring for the ill. She might also be expected to do piecework at home as part of the garment industry of the Lower East Side.

Laundry was a particularly arduous task for the immigrant mother in this period. She awoke on Monday morning to wrestle with the mound of clothes she had left soaking overnight. Clothes and bedding had to be rinsed, scrubbed on a large washboard, anchored in a galvanized iron tub, rung out, boiled on the cast-iron stove, rung out again, and hung out on the clotheslines stretching from an apartment window to a pole in the backyard. To accomplish all this, many gallons of water first had to be carried into the apartment from a street hydrant. The job required a full day of extremely hard labor.

A male worker in the garment industry found it almost impossible to earn enough annually to care for a large family since the work was seasonal as well as low-paying. Generally, it took two or three wage earners to keep a family fed and housed. The family might have to put young children to work; children who had reached school-leaving age—fourteen in the 1920s—were sent out to find employment in the factories and shops. Both my parents had jobs at age fourteen. My mother found work in a book bindery. My father tried unsuccessfully to apprentice in the fur trade as a cutter, but since the older workers refused to teach him their craft for fear of competition, he wound up peddling candy in the evenings outside theaters on Second Avenue or Fourteenth Street.

Single young women like my mother soon made enough money from working in factories to exert some degree of independence if they were strong enough to do battle with patriarchal family values. Holding back some of their earnings for cosmetics and clothes was grudgingly allowed because young women had a challenge more important than their jobs: they had to find husbands, preferably with good jobs and some savings. The new immigrant girl often worked as a domestic in middle-class German-American Jewish households, but since the girls were often exploited financially and sexually, that type of work was despised. With a slight command of English and some developing skill (like the ability to handle a sewing machine), a young woman could quickly move into the industrial work force and earn much higher wages and some degree of prestige.

Although most single young women could see how marriage and childbearing resulted in progressive disempowerment, the social pressure to marry and have children drove them into the very domestic service in their own home that they had tried to avoid in the workplace. The profession of marriage broker (shadkhen—as a child I thought the word was "shotgun") was a lucrative one on the Jewish Lower East Side. A female cousin of mine who had reached spinsterhood (mid to late twenties) was matched up sight unseen with a wealthy, older Jewish man living in South America. She was pretty and well liked, especially by us children. My mother felt sorry for her since the groom, judging from the photo, was short, stocky, and bald (just like my dad). The marriage, however, was a fabulous success, resulting in happiness for both parties and producing several talented children.

The power of the single young woman to manage her own finances was much feared by parents and resented by the patriarchal community. Censure took the form of rabbis warning against the dangers of vanity, self-indulgence, and sexual freedom in person and in print, all of which was generally ignored by young Jewish women.

Young men and women both gained power within the family when they attended school in New York City. They learned English faster and better than their parents. Married immigrant women learned the new language last of all in the family. Although my grandmother lived in New York City for over fifty years, she never had more than a minimal command of English. Yiddish was almost exclusively her spoken language. Schoolchildren taught their parents English, which gave them a certain degree of power.

Single men had less leeway, especially the first-born son. He had to continue to help support the family until he married, which was also a Jewish duty. Since marriage was only possible with some financial independence, it often came very late for men. Commonly men in their late thirties married young women in their late teens or early twenties. Even after marriage, men were expected to continue to provide financial aid for their parents and younger siblings if needed.

The typical patriarchal father toiled long hours and, if religious, spent additional time in prayer at home or in the synagogue. In a sense, the synagogue was a place of refuge for beleaguered Jewish family men, just as the corner bar was for the Irish immigrant father—a refuge from nagging and derision by disappointed and sometimes desperate wives. Some Jewish men used religion as a way of avoiding work. By giving all their time to religious study and prayer, they supposedly were doing God's work, and that was more important than helping to keep food on the table. That man lived a rather princely life, full of respect for his erudition and saintliness, while his wife, daughters, and sons worked to keep him nonproductive. When a family had saved the small amount needed to go into the pushcart business, it was often the wife who did the selling while the husband "studied."

Education

At first young immigrants got jobs through relatives and friends. Public vocational schools located in the settlement houses also helped prepare young immigrants for the workforce. German American Jews tried to help their co-religionists by establishing employment agencies. Financial aid for vocational education and employment primarily served the garment industry. There workers had to be taught to operate sewing machines, cut fabric, make patterns, design, manufacture hats, treat and cut fur, and use dyes. They had to learn to work skillfully, of course, but they also had to learn to work fast. That requirement made factory work more hazardous than it ought to have been, but the pressure of competition was a constant factor in immigrant-staffed industries.

All young women were taught sewing at home, but the skills of a professional seamstress or dressmaker had to be learned from professionals. Many young people acquired training and skills in carpentry, printing, plumbing, and electrical work. Eventually the New York Public Schools offered advanced vocational education in specialized high schools. One of my uncles became a printer, while another became a master plumber thanks to available vocational education as well as on-the-job training.

Young European immigrant children and American-born children of immigrants were required by law to attend New York City public schools until they had reached a certain minimum age. In my parents' time children were required to remain in school until they either reached fourteen or finished the eighth grade. My mother received an eighth-grade certificate and then went to work to help support her family. My father reached fourteen and left school to join the workforce before finishing the eighth grade. My mother occasionally teased my father, claiming that she had more education than he did. After all, she had graduated from eighth grade.

New York City and New York State governments invested enormous sums of money to educate immigrants. Today the Lower East Side bears witness to public generosity during the peak immigration period in the form of a few surviving grand old school buildings whose rooftop sports facilities are enclosed (to keep children and balls from falling off). Architecturally sound, some still function as schools overflowing with the children of Hispanic and Chinese immigrants, while others serve as community centers and the like.

Immigrant children were bright but rowdy. All instruction was conducted in English, of course, with Irish Americans the usual teachers in the early part of the nineteenth century. The children sometimes broke out into Yiddish, to the exasperation of their teachers, and often mangled the English language. Slowly, in the 1920s and 1930s more and more Jewish teachers entered the school system. Discipline was strict. Children were required to sit silently, backs straight, while they were receiving lessons. The classes were coed except for certain subjects like gym, homemaking, and shop. Also, boys and girls used different school entrances and exits.

Teaching in the Lower East Side schools was not easy. Classes were large (as many as fifty pupils), children often were not clean, and sometimes a twelve-year-old immigrant would be found in the first grade, trying to learn English. Many immigrant children who came to New York City around the age of twelve or a little older never went to school. My father's older brother, Uncle Abie, who lived on the Lower East Side from the time he left Poland as an eight-year-old to his death at age ninety-four, never learned to read, and he could barely sign his name. Until well into his sixties he was employed as a loader of wagons and then trucks in the wholesale markets. He was, of course, very sensitive about his illiteracy, which was a great handicap. As a young man he had worked as a union teamster, that is, driving a team of horses pulling a freight wagon. When the transport industry was mechanized, he was unable to obtain a license to drive a truck because he could not read. I once asked

Uncle Abie if he had ever gone to school. He informed me that the authorities had tried to get him to stay in school and keep him there, but that he always managed to escape, disappearing for several days at a time.

Most Jewish children liked school, often loved their teachers, and were encouraged by their parents to do well. In the case of Uncle Abie, I fear Grandma was not able to give him much attention. She could barely handle a chronically unwell second husband, four sons, and an infant daughter.

Of course, there were some bigoted and sadistic teachers, but, by and large, New York City teachers were as sensitive, creative, and well prepared for their jobs as any teachers in the country. Naturally, they taught the three R's, but it seems that the most important subject was "Americanism." The melting-pot theory required that the immigrants become English-speaking citizens as soon as possible. Children were taught American history and what was then called "civics," that is, how the American government worked. Teachers taught good manners and personal hygiene. This was sometimes resented by immigrant children and their parents since facilities for washing one's whole body were often lacking and clean clothes were not always available at home. But in later years most children were glad for the inculcation.

The majority of Jewish elementary school pupils and those who went on to high school were probably no brighter than any other ethnic group. One thing that encouraged Jewish immigrant children to succeed in school was the fervent belief of most of their parents that education, leading to a professional life, was the ticket needed to escape from the ghetto and reap the rewards apparent to all who lived in the expanding metropolis of New York City.

Those children who managed to get more education prospered and were able to elevate their families to the lower middle class and relocate them to Brooklyn or the Bronx. Slowly immigrant family patterns began to conform to American class norms. Children regularly went to high school, and many high school graduates went on to City College of New York (for men) or Hunter College (for women). Early educational goals were modest: a teaching degree or a pharmacist's license.

Later aspirations for bright young men included medical, dental, or law degrees. Second-generation children looked beyond the city colleges to the Ivy League schools, but when Harvard University decided to limit Jewish enrollment in 1922, the New York City Orthodox community decided it was time to create a top-quality Jewish institution of higher learning. Yeshiva College (later Yeshiva University) had its origins in the 1915 merger of the Yeshivat Etz Chaim (founded in 1886) and the Rabbi Isaac Elchanan Theological Seminary (founded in 1896). Both institutions were located on the Lower East Side. Basically, a yeshiva's mission is to teach the tenets of Judaism as well as secular subjects, the former in a synagogue. Interestingly, in 1927 the main center was not built on the Lower East Side but in the Washington Heights section of upper Manhattan, presumably because the donors felt that the Lower East Side was too rough, too radical, too ghettolike, and less accessible than other possible locations in the city. The Lower East Side no longer represented Jewish America in the way middle-class, upwardly mobile Jewish Americans wanted to be represented or viewed. Yeshiva College was intended as a symbol of Jewish achievement and recognition in the entire country, not just New York City. Significantly, it is located not far from both Columbia University and City College of New York—and it overlooks that great American river, the Hudson. The middle-class Jewish neighborhood where Yeshiva College was originally built has changed entirely and now has only a very small residual Jewish population. The neighborhood currently is home to a very large population of new immigrants from the Caribbean and Central America.

Although German Jews established several Reform congregations and constructed synagogues on the Lower East Side in the mid-nineteenth century—the most famous of which was Congregation Emanu-El, built on Grand Street in 1845—the Jewish Reform movement also needed a first-rate educational institution. It established the Jewish Institute of Religion on West Fourth Street in 1922 for the instruction and preparation of Reform rabbis. The seminary would later move uptown and merge with Hebrew Union College. Congregation Emanu-El eventually moved uptown to Fifth Avenue and Sixty-fifth Street and remains the largest Jewish place of worship in the world.

With a solid education and parental and community support, plus excellent higher-education opportunities based on ability, a great number of immigrant Jewish children and their children grew up to make significant contributions to American society in a myriad of fields.

Work

Jews who came to America between 1882 and 1924 joined the expanding American labor force. Most became urban workers. In fact, just about everyone worked for wages, including grandparents, parents, single women, single men, and children. Mothers with small children kept house in crowded, unsanitary apartments. As was noted, they prepared meals, did wash by hand, nursed frequently ill children and adults, and either took in piecework or shared pushcart labor with their husbands to add to the family income.

At one time or another almost all immigrant households accommodated boarders. From my earliest childhood memory to the age of eleven, another adult lived with my family. In our case they were relatives who needed care and/or housing. My mother's mother, Grandma Bella, an invalid, lived with us and was cared for by both my parents until she succumbed at age fifty-nine, the result of more than twenty years of physical labor as a tenement janitor. A young widow with three children, she had no marketable skills when her tailor husband, my grandfather, died of tuberculosis (the "tailor's disease"), so all she could do to earn a living was clean hall toilets, wash floors, empty trash cans, and pull ashes from the furnace.

As soon as Grandma Bella died, her younger son, Uncle Charley, moved in with us—we always had a two-bedroom flat that could accommodate up to six people. Orphaned, Charley had no place to live. He came in his late teens and remained my roommate until the age of twenty-one, when he was drafted into the army in 1941 and was severely wounded in the battle for New Guinea in 1942. After the war he lived with us until his marriage. My mother fed and cared for all unstintingly—and helped at the candy stand too.

Male immigrants who had no specialized skills and who spoke no English joined the workforce at the lowest levels. Some single men became pack peddlers, who purchased dry goods, trinkets, nostrums, and patent medicines at wholesale prices on Division Street and then walked through the backyards of the tenements, all the while calling out their wares to housewives, who would invite them to their flat if they desired to make a small purchase. These men needed very little capital to start their minuscule businesses. Almost at their economic level—nearly beggars—were the street musicians, who performed in the backyards below the laundry lines for the penny wrapped in a piece of newspaper thrown down to them by a compassionate housewife. And then there were the individuals who also worked the yards to buy worn garments that they would resell to the rag merchants on Division Street.

Some enterprising peddlers lugged enormous packs aboard trains bound for upstate New York, New England, and even the South, selling their goods to farmers' wives and in villages and towns where they were welcome. A few of these men found such places to their liking and brought their families there and set up small dry goods, clothing, and furniture stores—or even junkyards. Their grandchildren would go on to become highly respected business and civic leaders in their communities. Their professionally educated great-grandchildren, in turn, left these small towns and moved to New York, Chicago, or Los Angeles.

Married men who could not or would not leave their families behind and who lacked marketable skills turned to the famous, entry-level, small-business opportunity: the pushcart. Women did this too. A cart would be rented, pushed to a food or dry goods wholesaler in the predawn, and then taken to a favorite spot on the streets, where amid fierce competition the peddler tried to sell his wares—usually food—before it spoiled.

Pushcart peddling was an all-weather job. Immigrants fought each other for prime spots on the busiest thoroughfares, like Hester Street. Some streets were permanently blocked with pushcarts until, under Mayor Fiorello H. La Guardia—who served as mayor from 1934 to 1945 and is remembered and beloved by my vast extended family as the only Republican they ever voted for—the indoor Essex Street Market was built. It not only relieved some of the pushcart congestion but also provided for food inspection and running water, plus required sanitation, thus cleaning up a portion of the Lower East Side food supply. The Essex Street Market is still in operation today. With enough capital saved and, if possible, with loans from relatives (never banks), a grocery or candy store could be bought and run from 6 A.M. to near midnight, with all family members helping out.

Young women without English and still in their Eastern European clothes, like my widowed paternal grandmother, could find work in service to slightly more affluent Jewish families, where they did the household chores and cooked. With some knowledge of English they could find work sewing in the garment-industry sweat-shops, where, although working conditions and pay were terrible, they could make enough money in season to buy some fashionable clothing and put aside some for a dowry. Men also worked in the garment industry as machine operators and owned their own sewing machines, which they carried to work each day; since they never could be sure that there would be work at this shop that day, to have their machines locked up spelled economic disaster.

Children helped their mothers with piecework, trimming cloth or carting bundles to and from the sweatshops. Girls, of course, did household chores so their mothers could sew by hand, make artificial flowers, or operate machines. If the family had any kind of a small business, all chipped in.

From the age of eight I helped my father by substituting for him at the candy stand for a few minutes at a time so he could go down to the basement toilet to relieve himself. I also sold early-evening editions of both Yiddish- and English-language newspapers in Seward Park; the penny profits went into the business coffer. On Sundays I carried my homemade shoeshine kit to East Broadway and shined shoes for a nickel a pair. This money I was allowed to keep.

The hardest thing I had to do for my parents was to take a weekly order for boxed candy to a wholesaler on Stanton Street, about a dozen streets from our candy and newspaper stand on Jefferson Street, corner of Henry Street, and pick up two small towers of candy boxes secured with coarse packing twine. Although they were extremely heavy, I had to carry these back home. The twine cut into my palms and fingers so badly that I had to stop at every street to rest. How I dreaded that task. But it had to be done. My older brother was gone, my sister was too young, my mother could not have done it, and pop had to tend the store. I never cried nor complained. He made many hikes to wholesalers north of Delancey Street, bringing back much heavier bundles than I could ever have dreamed of handling.

During one of pop's wholesaling trips a family tragedy resulted. My father did all his business in cash—which was not unusual in those days—and had no checking account. Unfortunately, he liked to carry all his money in his wallet, which he kept in his hip pocket. I think it made him feel bigger than the owner of a newspaper and candy stand if he had a lot of cash on him. I saw the wallet often. It was thick and bound by a rubber band. Somehow he lost it at, or after leaving, a wholesaler's. He went back to look for it, searching the streets—all to no avail.

Two hundred dollars—a fortune at the time—were lost. This money was meant to pay the rent, purchase food, pay the electric bill, and purchase stock. There was only a bit of change left in the wooden till. He told my mother, who was terribly upset but did not blame him and sympathized as best she could. Later, out of earshot of my father, she told my sister and me, and then she broke down into tears. She didn't know how we would eat for the next several weeks. My father wore a grim expression for many days and worked extra hours. He never mentioned his folly to his children, but we obviously knew. I now think that he must have borrowed some money from his brothers to tide us over, or perhaps my mother got some from her brothers. Of course, my father bought another billfold and kept all his money in it.

Until I began to write this book, I never thought about or realized how much my father had suffered when we lived on the Lower East Side. First, he must have felt a deep sense of humiliation; after twenty-five years of backbreaking work, he was still at the immigrant's starting point. Second, running the stand was physically hard; he was exposed to the elements in all seasons. Lastly, he developed varicose veins from standing in one position for so many hours each day. I often saw his thin legs as he changed clothes. The veins looked like small Brussels sprouts on stalks. He had at least two operations on his legs, always returning to the job in a day or two and still in pain. Clearly he was a man determined to provide for his family—Depression or no—and that he did.

Initially the greatest employer of immigrant Jewish workers was the garment industry. As a national industry it was founded, for all practical purposes, by German Jewish immigrants of the 1840s, who initially concentrated their factories, showrooms, and shops on the Lower East Side, where they also lived. When they began to move uptown after the Civil War, they continued to conduct their manufacturing business near the docks of the immigrant ships, which provided the cheapest source of labor available in the city. Soon Eastern European Jews and Italians constituted almost the entire workforce for the industry. The goods were made on the Lower East Side, sold in shops on Broadway to the west and, after many years, in midtown department stores along Fifth and Lexington Avenues.

Clothing became one of the first mass-produced consumer items in the United States. With the development of the nation's vast rail network, Lower East Side immigrant salesmen traveled the country taking orders for their newly established wholesaling companies. When there was more work than any of the manufacturers could handle, they turned to contractors—Eastern European Jews who had been in the garment business for a while—to round up a temporary workforce, paying the workers substandard wages. The contractors, working on the narrowest profit margins, filled the manufacturer's orders without regard for the health or welfare of their employees.

Thus the sweatshop was born. It could be a storefront or an apartment where an entire family and its boarders toiled long hours and went hungry when the "busy season" had passed. Today it is the Asian and Latin American workforce in this country—and workers overseas producing clothing and sporting goods for the Euro-American markets—that are being exploited.

The abused workers, exploited as they were by their co-religionists, could get no succor from the powerless local rabbis. This powerlessness cost the rabbinate much respect. Eventually the workers realized that any appeal to morality had to be made through a political forum. It was the advance of socialist thought on the Lower East Side that led to the foundation of labor unions there and to the restoration of human dignity to immigrant workers. Indeed, the impetus for the organization of Jewish labor came from young Russian Jewish intellectuals who were drawn to the Lower East Side in search of a utopia but instead found a dystopia of overcrowded tenements, dirty streets, and ubiquitous sweatshops. It was not the Promised Land by any means, and the intellectuals were determined to organize the workers and change that rapacious world.

Other industries on the Lower East Side were a little more benign. In 1900 seventy bakeries served the Jewish community. The bakers toiled under terrible conditions. The bakeries were located in dirty, rat- and roach-infested cellars. Initially the ovens were primitive and dangerous. Eventually, following the passage of sanitation laws to clean up the food industry, the number of Jewish bakeries grew into the hundreds and spread throughout the city. Most important for the bakers, the work was year-round and the skill required translated into better wages. Grandma Anna worked in a bakery shortly after arriving in New York City, and all her subsequent life she baked great apple strudel and magnificent challah (loaves of rich, braided bread usually eaten on the Sabbath eve).

The first Yiddish-speaking union in America, the Russian-Jewish Workers' Union, was founded on the Lower East Side in 1885, coinciding with the rising tide of immigrants from Eastern Europe. In 1888 the United Hebrew Trades was founded; it consisted of many small unions with workers from various Eastern European countries who had joined together for mutual support.

Making cigars was a major Lower East Side industry from the start, second only to the garment industry in terms of the number of workers it employed. At first rolling cigars was a highly skilled handicraft. Even after machinery was introduced, small cigar shops managed to survive on the Lower East Side, continuing to roll their cigars by hand. My father, a lifelong cigar smoker, had a favorite shop owned by a friend named Tom Lauria, a white-haired Italian American man in his fifties. On Saturdays my father took me to his shop. I remember the rich smell of fermenting tobacco and Mr. Lauria sitting behind the counter, arrayed with his knives and molds, rolling pieces of tobacco into the leaf wrappers and sealing the cigars—all the while carrying on a nonstop conversation with my father.

I think Tom Lauria lived alone at the back of his shop. Many small-business people lived at the back of the shop, separated only by a curtain. The mysterious Chinese people in their ubiquitous laundries seemed to this child to be always eating with chopsticks from bowls held close to their mouths. I glimpsed them when the curtains parted as someone entered or left the rear cubicle.

One time my father took me to the cigar shop with his friend Sheer Licht, a small-time boxing promoter with a cigar always in a corner of his mouth and a wide-brimmed hat pushed back on his head. He spoke with the cigar in place, his hands waiving in two-quarter time. Pop said that Licht once "owned a piece" of a light-weight African American contender. I remembered the name when, many years later, I read that this boxer, who had fought over a hundred fights, wound up shining shoes in Atlanta.

With the arrival of manufacturing equipment, cigar-making became less skilled, but working conditions and wages were still better than in most other Lower East Side industries since cigars were bought and smoked by men year-round, in good times and bad. Samuel Gompers, a great national labor leader, arose from this industry. A cigar maker like his father, Gompers ascended to the presidency of the Cigar Makers Union, led them out of the faltering Knights of Labor, and helped found the American Federation of Labor (AFL), which he led for thirty-seven years. Under Gompers labor unions grew in number and gained the respect of the American public. By 1914 there was little need for exclusively Jewish unions. For example, that year thousands of Jewish house painters were integrated into the AFL's Brotherhood of Painters.

New York City has always run on patronage. When immigrant Jews learned that they could vote once they had been granted citizenship, they rushed to file the necessary papers. They voted in a block—and almost always for Democratic candidates. New York City patronage city jobs fell their way as a matter of course. It seemed to me, as a child, that all public-service areas were staffed by certain ethnic groups: all the sanitation workers were middle-aged Italian Americans with great mustaches; the police were exclusively huge, red-faced Irish Americans; the older schoolteachers and

27

administrators were Irish or Anglo, while the younger ones were Jewish—often Hunter or City College graduates. Jews did not secure national patronage jobs until the FDR administration, the reason being that Republican administrations of the early twentieth century after Theodore Roosevelt had little interest in or concern for Democratic Lower East Side Jews.

The Triangle Shirtwaist Company Fire and the Rise of Labor Laws

The building that once housed the infamous Triangle Shirtwaist Company (a shirtwaist was a woman's blouse) is now part of New York University in Greenwich Village. The ten-story building is at the corner of Washington Place and Greene Street. Wall plaques relate the site's history and its significance in terms of organized labor's struggle for better working conditions for New York City workers in particular and American workers in general.

The top three floors of the commercial loft building housed the Triangle Shirtwaist Company. On Saturday, 25 March 1911, six hundred workers were jammed into those floors. Most were either immigrant Jewish or Italian young women or the daughters of immigrant Jews or Italians, ranging in age from thirteen to twenty-three. Workers at this typical garment-industry site were surrounded by piles of cloth, swirls of trimmings on the floors, and floating bits of thread and dust in the air. The ventilation was inadequate. Furthermore, because of the insufficient number of emergency exists, there was no way quickly to evacuate the upper floors of the building.

At five in the afternoon a fire broke out on the ninth floor. An updraft caused the fire to spread quickly to the tenth floor. The top of the building became an inferno. Girls ran to the elevators and the stairwell, but the exit doors had been locked by supervisors to prevent workers from slipping away before quitting time. Eventually some workers broke through the doors and reached the street. Others made their way to the roof, only to plunge to their deaths. Still others—like soldiers in an absurdly futile cause—were overcome by smoke and died at their machines.

The Fire Department was at the scene within minutes, but the equipment could not reach the upper floors, and when the girls began to jump from windows and the roof, the firemen's nets could not break the long fall. The girls fell like game birds, their screams echoing after them. When they hit the pavement, they instantly became lifeless piles of blood-red clothes. In a little over two hours the holocaust was over, with 125 young women and 21 men dead. Most of the dead were Jewish. Shocked, the entire Lower East Side went into deep mourning. None of the factory or building owners were punished since they had broken no laws.

Out of the ashes of the Triangle Shirtwaist Factory there arose a very powerful labor union, the International Ladies' Garment Workers Union (ILGWU), which had first come into being in the late nineteenth century as the International Cloak Makers' Union and adopted its present name in 1900. In 1909 Local 25 of the union embarked on a fourteen-week strike known as "The Uprising of the 20,000." Young female garment workers struck for better working conditions and more pay. Ironically, many of the strikers were women who would eventually wind up at the Triangle Shirtwaist Factory in 1911. In the early twentieth century the ILGWU affiliated with the American Federation of Labor. One by one men's clothing unions joined with the ILGWU in the AFL. Labor unity was long in coming, but it finally did happen.

The ILGWU remained a major element in American socialism. Incorruptible and outspoken, it fought successfully for better labor laws, working conditions, and eventually won the eight-hour day for all American workers. The Triangle Shirtwaist Company fire made membership in the union not only a right but a duty of all workers in the industry. Many strikes ensued, but the unionization of almost the entire Jewish American workforce was underway. The momentum continued through the Depression and into World War II. After the war it went on, but there were now new workers in the sweatshops, bakeries, machine shops, and hospitals. Some were African Americans, more were Afro-Caribbean immigrants, but most were Americans from Spanish-speaking Puerto Rico. The work of the great socialist unions, the ILGWU and Local 1199, representing the Drug Store and Hospital Workers (my father's union after the demise of his candy stand) proudly continues.

The Public Forum: Jewish Newspapers and Periodicals

Jewish newspapers and periodicals were amazingly effective in reporting and affecting Jewish public opinion in the late nineteenth and early twentieth centuries in New York City. To some extent this was the case because the rate of illiteracy among Jewish immigrants was the lowest rate of all the groups from eastern and southern European countries. Almost all of the German Jews who came to America in the mid-nineteenth century were literate in German, and some even knew Yiddish. The Polish and Russian Jewish immigrants possessed varying degrees of literacy in various languages. Almost all Polish Jewish immigrant men could read and write in Yiddish and all read Hebrew; some could speak Polish; and some were fluent in German. Jewish women from Poland mainly spoke Yiddish (though my grandmother, Anna, could converse in Polish as well as Yiddish). Generally they could also read Yiddish since the language is printed using Hebrew letters and women needed to read Hebrew in order, for example, to say the appropriate Sabbath blessings.

Male Jews who immigrated from the Vilna district of Russian-controlled Lithuania were often better educated (they were taught in Russian) than their brethren from other parts of the Russian Empire. Some of these men had to learn Yiddish on the Lower East Side. Jewish immigrants from other parts of the Russian Empire, such as Russian Poland (as distinct from Austrian Poland) were, for the most part, literate in Yiddish and sometimes even Hebrew if they had been exposed to a Talmudic education. A small percentage of Russian Jewish immigrants were illiterate and, on the whole, less skilled in marketable crafts than other Jewish immigrants from Eastern Europe.

In the 1880s, which marked the beginning of the massive emigration from Eastern Europe, a dozen Yiddish newspapers came into existence, although most had brief life spans of from one to four years and a readership of fewer than five thousand. One newspaper survived and succeeded by devouring its competitors: the *Yiddishe Gazetten,* founded in 1874, was the largest-circulation Jewish newspaper at the beginning of the twentieth century. At that time over 150 Jewish papers and periodicals were being published, and the intellectual quality of many of the periodicals was extremely high. The *Yiddishe Gazetten* lasted until 1928.

The most popular early periodical was the *New Yorker Yiddishe Volks-Zeitung,* which was published from 1886 to 1889. The *Freie Gesellshaft,* a distinguished Yiddish anarchist periodical, appeared from 1895 to 1914. In the first two decades of the twentieth century Yiddish-language specialized periodicals flourished. Among the subjects covered were politics, theater criticism, film criticism, music criticism, religious issues, labor activities, poetry, chess, humor, and—surprisingly for the time—women's issues. Clearly, there was a substantial intellectual immigrant core living on the Lower East Side.

The first Yiddish-language daily to succeed—although some days it never made it to press—was the *Yiddishes Tageblatt,* which appeared from 1885 to 1928. The first successful Yiddish morning daily, the Orthodox *Morgen Zhournal,* began publication in 1901. It sold very well at my father's stand and was generally bought for its copious want-ad section. Its competitors were the *Forward* (*Forverts* in Yiddish) the great socialist paper, which is still published as a weekly rather than a daily, and the less ideological and quite literary *Der Tog* (The Day). The *Mogen Zhournal* declined in the 1940s, and in the early 1950s it was absorbed by *Der Tog,* which had been founded in 1914 and lasted until 1972.

The last surviving Yiddish-language newspaper, the *Forward,* founded in 1897, was the most influential Jewish newspaper in America. It was and remains the newspaper of Abraham Cahan, the greatest Jewish American journalist and the first major Jewish American writer of fiction. When its daily national circulation approached two hundred thousand in the second decade of the twentieth century, the *Forward* was recognized as an arbiter and shaper of Jewish opinion for the entire country. It made the Lower East Side the capital of American Jewry for fifty years. It influenced Yiddish literature, Jewish American literature, the Yiddish theater, the nascent Yiddish film industry, New York City and American politics, the anticommunist direction of American socialism, and American justice.

The *Forward,* partly through its famous *Bintel Brief* (Bundle of Letters) columns—which consisted of letters from readers requesting advice and answers by staff editors—was a primer for immigrant adjustment. The *Forward* fought for the rights of workers. American Jews were proud of the newspaper, and many a Jewish American family living far from the Lower East Side, although reading the local English-language papers of their cities and towns, continued to subscribe and read the *Forward* for generations as a matter of pride and because it made them feel a little more "at home." That feeling was partly the result of the newspaper's location on the Lower East Side, where their grandmas and grandpas had lived. The Jewish community in America would today be more shallow, fractured, and disparate were it not for the appearance for over a century of the *Forward*.

Even early in the twentieth century Lower East Side Jews whose English was progressing began turning to the leading English-language newspapers of New York City for information. William Randolph Hearst's *New York Journal* and *New York American,* and Joseph Pulitzer's *New York World* were popular with Jewish readers because of their anticorruption campaigns. Hearst was so eager for a Jewish readership that in 1904 he published the short-lived Yiddish newspaper the *Yiddisher Amerikaner.* Later, Jews who patronized English-language papers preferred the *New York Times* or two very popular tabloids, the *New York Daily News* and the *New York Daily Mirror.*

Reading

Secular book publishing was slow to make headway on the Lower East Side before World War I. One problem was that while immigrants read a variety of foreign languages—including Yiddish, Russian, German, Hungarian, Polish, and Hebrew—relatively few read English. Also, various ethnic newspapers and periodicals regularly serialized fiction and nonfiction, so the few pennies spent for the daily paper provided the pleasures of literature and history. For decades the *Forward*'s famous *Bintel Brief* columns provided a running soap opera in print and was a wellspring of useful information. In short order newspaper readers found the works of Sholom Aleichem, Mendele Mocher Sforim, and I. L. Peretz in the pages before them. The great international Yiddish writer Sholem Asch appeared on the scene. Later many works by Isaac Bashevis Singer, who was to win the Nobel Prize in literature, and by his older brother, Israel Joshua Singer, first appeared in the *Forward*.

Early on, Yiddish romance novels, adventure stories, and thrillers were being published and selling well. Many were translations from Russian or German. Founded before the turn of the twentieth century, the Hebrew Publishing Company was formed to publish Yiddish classics (generally in pirated editions) and nonfiction works. The first English-Yiddish dictionaries published on the Lower East Side came out just before World War I. Finally, the International Library Publishing Company began to produce high-quality translations of world classics in Yiddish. A monumental event in terms of Jewish scholarship and pride was the publication of the twelve-volume *Jewish Encyclopedia* in 1912.

Originally the Educational Alliance (formerly the Hebrew Institute) housed the Aguilar Free Library. Then public libraries with substantial holdings began to be turned into free circulating libraries when the New York Free Circulating Library's eleven branches merged with the New York Public Library in 1900. The $5.2 million gift of Andrew Carnegie for the construction of library buildings was a great boon for all New Yorkers—especially immigrants, who lacked the money to buy books but were eager to read and improve themselves. The Astor Library on Lafayette Street, a long walk from East Broadway, begun in 1849, held over twenty thousand volumes and, although not a circulating library, was an important resource for immigrant students and intellectuals. (Its collection is now part of the New York Public Library's research division on Fifth Avenue and Forty-second Street.) Other free circulating libraries soon appeared on the scene. By 1900 all circulating libraries in lower Manhattan had significant Jewish and Slavonic collections.

Of particular importance to me is the branch of the New York Public Library next to Seward Park on East Broadway. Erected in 1910, it is a grand Renaissance-style edifice. It was *my* library, only two streets from my Henry Street home. Four or five generations of Lower East Side youngsters came there to have books read to them, learn to read, and begin to acquire a love and respect for books, an appreciation of the wisdom, knowledge, and beauty contained within their covers.

Religion and Secularism

In 1920 there were about five hundred Jewish congregations on the Lower East Side. Some were located in glorious synagogues, like the Eldridge Street Synagogue—the first on the Lower East Side designed for and built by Eastern European Jews—or the Pike Street Shul, while others were located in former churches. The overwhelming number resided in street-level stores or tenement apartments. Whereas the great synagogues had huge congregations, the storefront and apartment shuls scraped by with a few families and a part-time rabbi. Many of the larger congregations consisted of people from the same European country or province; in the early years Jews on the Lower East Side tended to cluster into subdistricts based on country, province, town, or village of European origin.

It would seem that the Lower East Side was a very religious place. Indeed, even in my time (the late 1930s and early 1940s) a profound silence engulfed the neighborhood from sundown on Friday to sundown on Saturday in observance of the Jewish Sabbath. Self-appointed Orthodox religious "police," bearded men in black coats and hats, would watch my father's stand to make sure he did not stay open a minute after sundown on Friday, ready to harass him if he dared to try to earn a few more cents for his family. In truth, the Lower East Side became less and less religious as the first-generation adult immigrants died or moved away. Even before World War I the religious zeal on the Lower East Side had begun to wane. The Jewish girls who died in the Triangle Shirtwaist Company fire worked on Saturdays, and since the building is located in Greenwich Village, most would have used public transportation, thus violating the strictures against travel on the Sabbath.

Although my paternal grandmother Anna was very religious, none of her five children were. My father was never a member of an East Side congregation, although he did generally manage to attend services somewhere on the High Holy Days. My mother journeyed with her parents from London to Harlem when she was about ten years old. Her parents were not religious and she never attended a synagogue, although, surprisingly, she lighted Friday-evening candles and the annual memorial lamps for her dead parents.

I suspect that although the majority of my parents' generation respected the religious immigrant Jews and even supported religious institutions with modest contributions, they were quite content to leave the maintenance of the religion to a truly devout minority. The latter provided the cultural constant. It was comforting to see old rabbis passing by and synagogues on every street. If queried, my relatives identified themselves as Orthodox—never Conservative or Reform—Jews, but this was just a badge of identification to be worn on some family occasions, especially bar mitzvahs and funerals. Poor as they were, socialism, radicalism, anarchism—let alone apostasy—were not for them, although socialism had attracted huge followings in the immigrant Jewish community a generation before. No one advocated assimilation, but I suppose their true religion was Americanism. Their faith was in America. Their hope was to make a little money.

My father spent part of his hard-earned family income to send me to an after-school Talmud Torah class for a year prior to my bar mitzvah to learn how to read (but not to understand) enough Hebrew in order to recite a portion of the Torah at the ceremony. I was also taught by an elderly sexton at an East Broadway synagogue to put on tefillin, the prayer phylacteries, which, along with all my male friends, I did for a short time after my bar mitzvah and then stowed them away, together with my prayer shawl and prayer book, forever. My friends and I found Orthodox services raucous, rude, chaotic, irreverent, rushed, babbling, and bordering on parody. They seemed all form and little substance, full of sound yet lacking in soul.

Prostitution

Prostitution had long existed openly in Eastern European cities. Jews, too, were customers, procurers, and sex workers. During the Eastern European migration period many married immigrant men came to New York City initially without their wives. Like many unmarried men, they sometimes resorted to prostitutes for sexual gratification. The heyday, so to speak, of prostitution on the Lower East Side was the period from 1890 to 1914. Allen Street, filled with tenements in generally poor condition and nestling in the shadow of the elevated rail system (commonly referred to by New Yorkers as the El), was a logical place for brothels, as was Forsyth Street. Prostitutes could also be seen plying their trade on the main crosstown streets, like Delancey and Houston, and, of course, on the Bowery.

Most, but not all, of the women in "the life" on the Lower East Side were poor Jewish immigrants or children of immigrants who chose this dangerous way of making a living over domestic service or the sweatshop. The wages were certainly better, and many were supporting families in the old country or loved ones in New York. Some women ended up committing suicide, while others became diseased, alcoholic, or addicted to drugs. Despite pressure from pimps and the politicians they bribed, some managed to leave the trade, find husbands, and blend into the "respectable" life of the community. Frequently trumped up "White Slave" scandals boosted newspaper circulation and energized social reformers. Relatively few of these women were actually tricked into the trade.

At one time steerage-class young women arriving at Ellis Island had to be met by a relative before they were released—such was society's fear of White Slavery (a racist term referring to the trade in nonblack female bodies for prostitution; it didn't seem to matter much if African American women or Chinese immigrant women were bought and sold). Law enforcement, police raids, and reformers' zeal usually led to a rise in the cost of a prostitute's services but did little to stem the tide in the trade. The practice of holding young women at Ellis Island until a bona fide relative showed up of course amounted to discrimination by gender. The young immigrant woman didn't need protection as much as she needed financial help, an initial safe residence, and vocational training. These were often provided by Jewish charitable organizations.

I first learned about prostitution when I was eleven from a book in my father's small bookcase by Mike Gold entitled *Jews without Money* (1930). It shocked me for two reasons. First, the title seemed tautological in that I didn't think there were any Jews *with* money. Second—and more profound—was the idea that women's bodies were once for sale on the *Jewish* Lower East Side. This was shocking to me because, until we moved from Henry Street to the Bronx in 1944, I never saw or knew of any woman who was—or even looked like—a prostitute. Clearly, that was because the city of my childhood was Mayor La Guardia's New York. His reforming influence lasted for several years until New York City returned to business as usual. In his great cleanup of city corruption and vice, the "Little Flower" successfully drove prostitution off the streets and made it very difficult for bordellos to operate.

I did know about sex. I first learned about it at age eleven from a friend while we sat on a street curb. His revelations were quickly confirmed by a precocious younger (!) female cousin. Typical for the time, my parents never mentioned, let alone discussed, sex with me. As far as I could surmise, they were still virgins (not *my* mother!).

However, during regular searches of my father's possessions, at the back of a little drawer at the top of his clothes chest I discovered a palm-sized viewer with peepshow-type slides of a woman and a man coupling. I made frequent trips to the titillating cache to further investigate the sex act, but I must have visited the site once too often because one day, barely two weeks after my serendipitous discovery, the viewer had disappeared.

Under La Guardia the city was literally cleaned up. Sanitation services improved. Vice was out. Burlesque was banished to Union City, New Jersey. Slot machines were hunted down and destroyed, often documented in a photo showing the little mayor smashing them with an ax. Other gambling activities were attacked and, as I said, prostitution went underground. The open prostitution that Michael Gold describes in *Jews without Money* just did not exist in the La Guardia period. In fact, later in my youth a teenage friend hitchhiked all the way to Montreal and back to find a prostitute in order to lose his virginity. He succeeded, and the rest of us pals demanded all the details.

Other Types of Crime

Early in the twentieth century, New York City police officials and reformers both believed that Jews were more prone to criminality than other people, especially native-born citizens (which the immigrant population referred to as Yankees). In the 1910s one police commissioner, lacking any genuine statistical evidence, claimed that half of New York City's criminals were Jewish.

In fact, Jews were much more frequently the victims of crime rather than the perpetrators. The Irish gangs that roamed the Five Points section of lower Manhattan—near City Hall—in the mid-nineteenth century still controlled much of the New York underworld. At the end of the nineteenth century Italian gangs were challenging them. Chinese gangs quickly took control of Chinatown and were permitted to operate in their own area by the older gangs and the police. African Americans had no organized-crime mobs. Like immigrant Jews, they were more often victims than perpetrators. The unsavory Bowery and the docks bordered the Lower East Side. A favorite and easy victim of a felonious sailor or Irish gang member was an old, bearded Jew, who was usually taunted and then robbed.

In the 1930s and 1940s Jewish criminals did become junior members of Italian gangs as the Mafia took over organized crime from the Irish in the city. Murder Inc. was an illegal Jewish protection gang led by Louis "Lepke" Buchalter. The notorious criminal buddies Benjamin "Bugsy" Siegel and Meyer Lansky were well integrated in the Mafia. But New York Jews never created or worshiped "godfathers." Criminal life was always shameful to families and communities. Those who had entered the criminal world—usually through illegal gambling—were almost never boastful or proud of what they were doing. For some crime was a way of combating the poverty that they and their families endured. To my knowledge there were no second-generation Jewish criminals. That is, a criminal father—usually involved in gambling or, in the Prohibition era, the illegal importation and selling of liquor—shielded his family from the "business" as best he could, sending his children on to college and the various professions. Some contemporary sociologists have claimed that Jewish criminals inspired Jews to be less passive and more willing to fight to protect body and property. I believe this theory to be incorrect. Jewish gangsters were despised, not looked upon as heroes to be emulated.

As I stated earlier, there were Jewish prostitutes. Although the community was deeply ashamed of the fact, there was no organized violence against them, only a refusal to accept them as members of the community. Rarely did Jews commit crimes of passion. A Jewish murder case was a shocking event in the ghetto. There were Jewish burglars and extortionists, pimps, and muggers. Young men, overly anxious to get some money, became petty thieves. Pilfering from pushcarts was a sport. The local thieves were not honored by the community. In fact, they generally were treated as pariahs.

More than most New Yorkers Jews turned to and trusted the police, but they were often disappointed. To obtain equality under the law, they realized that they had to become lawyers, judges, and policemen as soon as possible, which they did. My father's youngest brother, Uncle Artie, became a New York City Police Department detective in the late 1930s.

The Impact of Historical Events

Certain major historical events that coincided with the 1882–1924 immigration period galvanized the Jewish Lower East Side. One of the very first was the infamous Dreyfus Affair, which began in 1894 in supposedly liberal, republican, democratic France. Alfred Dreyfus, a French army captain, was falsely accused of betraying French military secrets to Germany. Dreyfus was a Jew. He protested his innocence. The evidence was flimsy and circumstantial. His handwriting looked a little like that of the actual (but then still undiscovered) spy. Bigoted army judges, eager to find a scapegoat, falsely found him guilty. France became engulfed in a wave of vicious anti-Semitism, which horrified Jewish communities around the world. Dreyfus was sentenced to public degradation, dismissal from the army, and life imprisonment in the dreadful prison colony of Devils Island, situated off the coast of French Guiana.

In 1896 Colonel Georges Picquart found evidence that the real spy was Major Ferdinand Walsin Esterhazy, an aristocrat. But Picquart was silenced by the embarrassed and bigoted general staff, which preferred to label an Alsatian-born Jew as the villain rather than a French aristocrat. In 1897 Dreyfus's brother also discovered the truth and demanded a new trial. France, now split into two factions, was again in turmoil, which lasted for ten years. One party, the anti-Dryfusards, consisted of royalists, the military, the Roman Catholic Church, and almost the entire Roman Catholic population of France. Synagogues were attacked and Jews were mobbed while right-wing newspapers dripped anti-Semitic venom. The anti-Dreyfusards at first prevailed by using patriotism and forgeries to convince the public of Dreyfus's guilt.

The Dreyfusards, the minority and less powerful party, consisted of socialists, republicans, and anticlericals. They were convinced of Dreyfus's innocence. Esterhazy was tried and acquitted. In 1898 the great French writer Émile Zola wrote an incendiary article entitled "J'accuse" in which he defended Dreyfus and attacked the army and the bigots of France. Arrested, tried, and sentenced to prison, he fled to England.

Later that year a Colonel Henry, who had forged evidence against Dreyfus in the Esterhazy trial, committed suicide, possibly because he feared arrest. The court of appeals ordered a new trial for Dreyfus, who was enduring a tortured existence in a tropical hell, all the time knowing that he was innocent. Back in France, to the surprise of justice-loving people the world over—and to the horrified dismay of the Jewish Lower East Side community—a military court again found Dreyfus guilty in 1899. Ashamed for his country, President Emile Loubet pardoned Dreyfus, but the case was not over.

The Dreyfusards fought on for exoneration and complete restoration of Dreyfus's rights. To them the very honor of France in the eyes of the world was at stake. In 1906 the Dreyfus case was at last tried in a civilian court, the supreme court of appeals, where Dreyfus was exonerated and returned to duty as a major. Dreyfus eventually retired as a lieutenant-colonel. The publication of certain German papers in 1930 conclusively established Dreyfus's innocence. The Dreyfus Affair so shamed the army, the monarchists, and the Catholic Church in France that it resulted in furthering the separation of church and state, greater civilian control of the military, and the rise of the Socialist Party.

The Dreyfus Affair in France and the shock and dread it evoked in Jews around the world also engendered one of the most significant historical movements of the mid-twentieth century, a nationalistic movement that would eventually unite world Jewry as never before. Initially, however, it seriously divided the Jews of the world.

After witnessing the railroading of Alfred Dreyfus and the explosion of anti-Semitism in France, Theodor Herzl, a Viennese journalist and a Jew, came to the conclusion that Jews could truly be safe only in a country of their own. In 1897 he called for the first World Zionist Congress to be held in Basel, Switzerland. The goal was to establish a Jewish homeland in Palestine, the biblical land of the Jews, then a department of the Turkish province of Syria, with a majority population of Arab-speaking Muslims and Christians.

In fact, Jews were already living in Palestine, especially in Jerusalem, and had been doing so since the time of Joshua. Some Jews had survived the genocides of the Romans and the Christian crusaders. Many religious Jews, supported by overseas charities, prayed daily at the Western Wall of the destroyed temple of Herod, the second Temple.

As a child I had often heard about the pious Jews living in the Jewish quarter of Jerusalem. My cousin Rosie, who was a little older than my mother, carried a charity box to all family functions and bludgeoned relatives into putting their coins into her collection box for the Sages of Israel in Jerusalem and elsewhere. A gadfly and a saint, she kept herself and her postal clerk husband poor so that elderly scholars could survive and continue their holy work. In addition, a few Jewish pioneers from Eastern Europe had already come to Palestine to farm, build, and begin the reconstruction of the homeland. The Turkish government and Arab landlords had sold land to them.

The establishment of the great Jewish nationalistic movement called Zionism caused heated debate, consternation, and division in the world Jewish community until 1933, when the German people embraced Hitler and the Nazi Party. With rising anti-Semitism around the world, the perplexing question arose: Were Jews merely members of an international religion like any other or were they a nation in exile? If the latter, given the possibility of a choice, where should Jews live?

From 1882 onward 1.5 million Polish, Ukrainian, Lithuanian, Russian, Hungarian, and Rumanian Jews poured into the open door that was America, a nation eager for their labor. Everywhere Hasidic rabbis had struggled to keep their congregations from emigrating to "godless" America. "Better to die poor but holy in Poland or Russia," they preached. Ironically, that is precisely where their congregations died.

Zionists argued that the safest choice for the Jewish people was to establish a homeland, a Jewish state, in Palestine, a small region where Jews would be in the majority for once in two millennia. In 1917, as World War I raged on, British Foreign Secretary Arthur Balfour issued what came to be known as the Balfour Declaration, which pledged British support for a Jewish national home in Palestine. Thus, a world power had concurred with the Zionist program.

Young Lower East Side Jews debated whether to undertake aliya, the return to the homeland. The socialist kibbutz movement looked attractive, especially during the Great Depression, but almost all Jews were content to stay in the countries of their citizenship, including Germany. Hitler made all Jews Zionists to the extent that they supported the establishment of Israel as a refuge for the survivors of the Holocaust. The belligerence of the Arab states following the division (1948) by the United Nations of the abandoned British mandate of Palestine into a Jewish and an Arab state confirmed world Jewry's belief in the need for the continued existence of the State of Israel. The argument over whether Jews should live in the Diaspora or in Israel is never-ending, but for almost every Jew in the world today the survival of Israel is of enormous significance.

The truths of the almost inconceivable dimensions of the Holocaust that came to light in 1945 naturally stunned American Jews in general and the Lower East Side in particular. The mourning was so deep—the vast majority of American Jews had roots (and often relatives) in those European countries where the Jewish populations were destroyed—that adults like those in our large extended family were shocked into silence.

I will never forget the first time I heard of a German atrocity. One day late in 1939 I was about to leave for elementary school. I was sitting in the basement kitchen on Henry Street when my mother's friend and neighbor, Mrs. Adler, a German Jewish refugee, rushed into the room in tears. She told my horrified mother that she had learned that her brother in Germany had been taken to a concentration camp by the Gestapo. When his wife inquired about his welfare, she was handed a cigar box containing his ashes. Thus, my first Holocaust nightmare was born.

Besides the Dreyfus trial, two other trials angered and frightened the Jewish people of the Lower East Side during this period. One occurred in Kiev, the Ukraine, in 1913. It involved a blood libel murder charge. In the Middle Ages most Christians believed that Jews killed Christian children in order to use their blood in Jewish rituals. It was pure slander, of course, but a murdered Christian child could provoke a general pogrom. A poor Jewish worker named Mendel Beiliss was arrested and falsely accused of murdering a Christian child in order to harvest its blood for ritual purposes. Yet another flood of anti-Semitism engulfed Russia. After a long imprisonment and trial, Beiliss was exonerated. In 1966 the writer Bernard Malamud used the Beiliss blood libel case as the basis for his novel *The Fixer*. Russian-born or not, most Lower East Side Jews hated the Russian Empire and, after the German-Russian nonagression pact of 1939, the Soviet Union as well.

The second infamous trial occurred in Atlanta, Georgia, in 1914. A Jewish businessman named Leo Frank was accused of the murder of a fourteen-year-old girl who had been working for him. Despite his declaration of innocence, he was found guilty of murder and was sentenced to death on the dubious evidence of one person, an employee named Jim Conley. It seemed to most Jews that if Frank were not Jewish, he would not have been so easily convicted. The streets of Atlanta echoed with the cry "Kill the Jew!" The governor of Georgia was very uncertain about the verdict and, wishing to avoid a fatal miscarriage of justice, commuted the sentence to life imprisonment. A lynch mob subsequently broke into the prison and murdered Frank.

The Lower East Side was in an uproar. Jewish newspapers, generally liberal and invariably against Jim Crow, had editorialized against the lynching of African Americans in the South and elsewhere. Now a Jew had been lynched. Doubts arose in Jewish minds: Was America a refuge from persecution after all? How different was it, really, from czarist Russia when it came to hatred and persecution of Jews?

The Dreyfus Affair in France, the Beiliss blood libel case in Russia, the Frank lynching in the American South, the rise of virulent anti-Semitism in Nazi Germany commencing in 1933, growing anti-Semitism in the United States in the 1930s, and, ultimately, the news of the Holocaust all contributed to the belief of American Jews that they, too, needed the security of a homeland.

The Yiddish Theater

The Lower East Side's immigrant Jews loved their Yiddish theater. It was both innocent and corrupt. Although it was often unpolished, unsophisticated, rude, gross, salacious, slapdash, mawkishly sentimental, melodramatic, and outrageously overacted, it was exuberant and vital. It reflected the immigrant's great concerns: the loss of religious faith and identity; the assimilation of their children through mixed marriages; the fear of poverty; the longing for loved ones left behind forever in Europe; the pain of anti-Semitism; the desire for justice; and the frustrations of trying to understand and cope with American society and values. One should also not forget the shameful ingratitude of children toward their parents—a favorite theme of Lower East Side Jews. The tired workers of an essentially proletarian community needed the passion, emotion, release, diversion, and comfort of the theater. The Yiddish theater shamelessly elicited tears from its audience, but it just as frequently made that same audience laugh—most often at themselves.

From its inception the American Yiddish theater was doomed. English-speaking second- and third-generation American Jews looked down upon it even if they retained a smattering of the Yiddish language. The subtleties were lost on them. For them it was greenhorn entertainment or simply shund (trash).

For most of the immigrant audience the experience of live theater was new. Although Jewish traditions included masquerading and playacting during the Purim holiday and tomfoolery at weddings and bar mitzvahs, an institutionalized Jewish theater existed in but a handful of Eastern European cities prior to the commencement of the great migration in 1882. Odessa, for example, had had a notable Yiddish theater tradition until the czar banned it in 1883. Although the Rumanian-born playwright Abraham Goldfaden (1840–1908) is acknowledged as the father of the professional Yiddish theater (he produced his plays in both his native country of Russia and in the United States), the professional Yiddish theater really developed in Eastern Europe and America simultaneously. Just like Yiddish literature, it crisscrossed the Atlantic. Interestingly, the birth of the Yiddish theater as a major cultural institution in America and in Europe coincided with the advent and development of realism in European drama. The playwrights and managers of the Yiddish theater were already aware of the significance of Ibsen and Chekhov early on.

The first Yiddish play productions in the 1880s were performed in makeshift halls with amateur actors, but a Yiddish star actor came to the forefront immediately. Ukrainian-born Boris Thomashevsky (1868–1939) was the Lower East Side's first matinee idol. However, a successful theater tradition also needs excellent playwrights. When a genuine if inconsistent talent for the new theater appeared in the person of Russian-born Jacob Gordin (1853–1909), real theater bloomed on the Lower East Side, with actors and dramatists now able to hone their respective crafts.

Among the Yiddish theaters were the Oriental, the Windsor, and the People's Theater (Thomashevsky's venue) on the Bowery, a street of varied forms of entertainment; the Rumanian Opera House on Second Avenue; the National on Second Avenue and Houston Streets; the Sunshine Theater on East Houston Street (now a multiplex cinema); the Anderson Yiddish Theater on East Fourth Street and Second Avenue; the Grand on its namesake (the venue for the second greatest Yiddish matinee idol, Russian-born Jacob P. Adler [1855–1926]); Poole's on Eighth Street; the Orpheum on St. Mark's Place and Second Avenue; and the Thalia on Fourteenth Street (the Lower East Side's upper geographical limit). Second Avenue also held the Public at Fourth Street and the Second Avenue Theater, which was built in 1909 for the outstanding character actor David Kessler (1859–1920), and was one of the Lower East Side's most opulent theatrical establishments. The number of Yiddish theaters in New York City rose to eighteen in 1920 and declined from then on.

As the twentieth century commenced, theatrical performances on the Lower East Side mushroomed to the point where over a thousand occurred each year, with the number of annual patrons exceeding one million. Admission was very cheap, and blocks of seats were often sold to organizations involved in fund-raising. Members were required to sell approximately ten tickets or pay for the seats themselves. My father regularly was given a handful of benefit seats to sell for his fraternal lodge and he seldom sold more than a pair or two. Moreover, as a small neighborhood businessperson, he had to buy tickets from his own customers. As far as I was concerned, the Sternlicht family went to the Yiddish theaters on Second Avenue far too frequently. As my Yiddish was very weak, I remember little of the experiences except admiring the beauty of the theater interiors, the fine clothing theatergoers wore—and being extremely bored. Like so many other children in the audience, I simply couldn't follow enough of the dialogue. All the plays seemed to be set in kitchens ruled by an overweight mother who screamed and cried a lot, unlike my mother.

In fact, the Yiddish Theater made no one rich except for a very few celebrity actor-managers. Still, the industry employed a lot of people and gave much pleasure to those whose first—or only—language was Yiddish. For a dollar hard-working people like my grandmothers, my parents, and my uncles and their wives, could put on their best clothes, go to a festive gathering, meet their friends in the audience, and be entertained almost as if they were "somebody." In their eyes it was a glamorous affair.

The golden age of the Yiddish theater occurred between the end of World War I (1918) and the beginning of World War II (1939). Yiddish theater matured during that period primarily due to a third larger-than-life actor and director/manager—Ukrainian-born Maurice Schwartz (1890–1960). He began the Yiddish Art Theater movement in the United States at the Irving Place Theatre, just off Fourteenth Street. Schwartz's backup was the fine actor Jacob Ben-Ami (1890–1977), an intellectual who eventually played and directed for the Theatre Guild and the Civic Repertory Theatre, both distinguished American companies. The Yiddish Art Theater, as Schwartz called his company, performed works by Schiller, Ibsen, Shaw, Tolstoy, Wilde, Strindberg, Sholom Aleichem, Sholem Asch, and S. Ansky (notably *The Dybbuk*). The non-Yiddish plays were, of course, translated into the first language of the audience. Schwartz moved his company to a theater on Second Avenue near Twelfth Street (now a multiplex cinema) that he renamed the Yiddish Art Theater, as his company was called. It was a proud institution that lasted until 1950, when a significant audience no longer existed.

For the most part Yiddish theater was an actor's theater. The popular repertory basically consisted of historical melodramas, costume operettas, improbable situation comedies full of asides and clowning, and tearful family tragedies. It was like the early silent films, only it had sound and color. Still, the Russian-born playwright Jacob Gordin (1853–1909) had introduced realism in Yiddish drama as early as 1890. A master of characterization, he reached his audience by writing about experiences they could easily have undergone. One of his earliest successes was *Siberia* (1891), which depicted the troubles of a young Russian Jewish man sentenced to exile in Siberia who managed to escape, change his identity, and become rich, only to be betrayed by a rival businessman. Gordin translated or "borrowed" plots, characters, and situations from Shakespeare, Ibsen, Hugo, and others. One of Gordin's greatest successes was *Der Yiddishe King Lear* (1892), with Lear transformed into a wealthy Russian Jewish patriarch; Jacob P. Adler achieved immortality with his portrayal of the patriarch. The play remained in the Yiddish theater repertory for a generation. I can remember relatives talking about the play even though none were old enough to have seen a production in Gordin's lifetime. Their verdict was that Gordin's tragedy was better than Shakespeare's! True realism, the staple of modern drama, only appeared on the Yiddish stage in translations of plays by Ibsen, Strindberg, and Chekhov—or through borrowings from their plots and characters.

My parents and their friends especially admired Molly Picon (1898–1992), the attractive tenement-born actress who had to learn Yiddish as a young woman in order to appear on the Yiddish stage, and Menasha Skulnik (1894–1970), the Polish-born stage comedian. They were in the front ranks of the final generation of Yiddish stage stars.

Lower East Side immigrants and their descendants were universally proud of those entertainers who had managed to escape from the ghetto and rise to stardom in American society. From the Yiddish theater came Paul Muni (Friederich Weisenfreund; 1895–1967), a graduate of the Yiddish Art Theater company and Broadway, who became internationally famous as a film actor; Edward G. Robinson (Emanuel Goldenberg; 1893–1973), one of film's great tough guys; and John Garfield (Jules Garfinkle; 1913–1952), a fractious leading man.

The great entertainer Al Jolson (Asa Yoelson; 1886–1950) was the son of a Lower East Side cantor. Jolson played a cantor's son in *The Jazz Singer* (1927), the first film with spoken dialogue. Other Jewish radio and television stars included Jack Benny (Benjamin Kubelsky; 1894–1974) and George Burns (Nathan Birnbaum; 1896–1996) of the Burns and Allen team. Lower East Side Jews knew that the playwright Clifford Odets's (1906–1963) radicalism came from his Jewish socialist background.

My Jewish entertainer-hero was radio and film comedian Eddie Cantor (Edward Israel Iskowitz; 1892–1964), a fellow alumnus of the Educational Alliance. I eagerly awaited his weekly radio show. I especially revered him for generously endowing a summer camp for poor ghetto kids. For several summers I got a chance to ride a real train—not a subway car—up into the Catskills and spend two weeks clowning around with other boys and batting mosquitoes.

Other Forms of Recreation and Entertainment

Besides the Yiddish theater and the nascent film industry, in the first decade of the twentieth century Lower East Siders participated in a large number of cultural activities, from lectures to social dancing in the settlement houses. Also, there were many social and political clubs. Labor-union halls provided forums for workers interested in improving working conditions. Coffee shops, small dairy restaurants, and cafeterias (like the Garden Cafeteria on East Broadway) were places for socializing. Two famous café venues on Second Avenue—the Jewish theater district—the Café Royal (on Twelfth Street) and the Café Monopole (on Ninth Street) brought fans and stars in close proximity.

Of course, there were also saloons on the Lower East Side. Quite a few had opened in the mid-nineteenth century when the area was largely Irish. Most of these bars were located on or near the Bowery (where burlesque, with its risqué routines and scantily dressed women, was another popular entertainment for men). A large part of the Bowery clientele came from outside the district.

Since excessive drinking was always frowned upon by Jews, in the initial immigration period relatively few bars served the enormous Jewish population. The business was just not there. The vast majority of patrons were men. As I recall, no female relative of my mother's generation ever took more than a sip of wine on a holiday, and that was always at home. No men frequented bars or went to them regularly to socialize. It just wasn't done. Male friends would share a bottle of whiskey, accompanied by bread, and interspersed with heated conversation around the kitchen table.

Women and men came together at dancing academies and dance halls. These proved to be popular places to meet members of the opposite sex in a community that provided few other opportunities except through a matchmaker. Mothers frowned upon the idea of their daughters patronizing such places, fearing that the girls would meet unacceptable males, but these objections were generally ignored.

Recreation for children was very limited. Most play activities occurred on the crowded streets. Boys living in an area with access to the East River—such as "Alphabet City" (Avenues A, B, C, and D)—could swim in the filthy river during the broiling hot summer. Tiny Seward Park, built in 1900, had a playground. During World War II children like me were given small parcels of land in the park to grow vegetables for the war effort. The soil was terrible. I grew only a few radishes—which I disliked—and gave up the little homestead after only one season.

Children really did not have much free time. Many worked after school, helping their parents. Jewish boys, almost without exception, also attended Hebrew school after public school and on Sundays—with attendance in the shul required on Saturday. Of course, the settlement houses provided some day care as well as educational and cultural activities for children.

In the summer there was a charity boat ride on the Hudson River for tenement kids, as well as the two-week summer-camp experience. The intolerable heat was also partially relieved when a parent—my mother, in my case—took the children to Coney Island. The subway and elevated ride seemed interminable. Arriving at ten in the morning, my mother, my sister, and I ran to the beach to stake out territory by spreading out grandfather's wool army blanket. Mother anchored the blanket and guarded our toys. Then it was off with our outer clothes—we already had our bathing suits on underneath—followed by a mad dash through the roosting throng of sunbathers and, screaming in anticipation of the cold, into the surf.

In the afternoon, beginning to feel sunburned, we packed up and headed for Nathan's Famous food emporium on Coney Island Avenue for hot dogs. Finally, the pièce de résistance: the rides, games, penny arcades, the mechanical horses in Steeplechase Park, and the bumper cars that I could have driven for the rest of my life. Then the sleepy, uncomfortable ride home in a hot, sweaty train, the crash of the waves and the screams of pleasure still ringing in our ears.

Unique for my generation of New York City dwellers was the most unforgettable, fantastic experience a child could possibly have, namely, a visit to the 1939 New York World's Fair! Different relatives brought me to the fair on several occasions both in 1939 and 1940. I think adults enjoyed the fair more with children along. To this day I mourn the loss of two treasured souvenirs, misplaced during one of several moves: my Heinz pickle pin and an imitation gold cigarette case shaped like an envelope, with a large World's Fair postage stamp in the upper-right-hand corner. The blue-and-white stamp illustrated the fair's famous symbols: the trylon and the perisphere. For some unknown reason—perhaps because he knew how much I had loved the fair—a favorite older cousin gave it to me in 1942, just before he went off to air combat and was grievously wounded.

Food

The nineteenth-century tenement flats had cast-iron stoves that served for cooking and heating. The stoves were dangerous. Soot fires in stovepipes occurred often. Children burned themselves on the red-hot iron stove top. As late as 1950 Grandma Anna had a cast-iron stove in her Norfolk Street kitchen. She also had a very small gas stove with an oven and four burners. Grandma preferred cooking and baking with the big stove, presumably because she had used one for forty years. Also, Uncle Abie brought her scrap wood for fuel from the market where he worked.

Refrigerators began to appear in Lower East Side flats in the late 1940s. On Madison Street and Henry Street we had iceboxes to keep food fresh. The iceman brought cakes of ice for the top compartment of the icebox. My job was to empty the drip pan at the bottom every morning. If I forgot and the water spilled onto the kitchen floor, I was in trouble.

Housewives worried about spoilage, especially in the summer. They shopped daily for what they hoped were fresh vegetables and fruit on the pushcarts and, later, in the Essex Street Market. Live chickens were selected in the east Delancey Street chicken market and given to the ritual slaughterer (schochet), who dispatched the bird with a swift stroke of his blade.

As is well known, Jewish cuisine is a product of the Diaspora and the Kashrut, the Jewish dietary laws. Since New York City Jewish immigrants mostly came from Germany, Poland, Russia, Hungary, Ukraine, Rumania, and Lithuania, the foods they ate were similar to that of their gentile neighbors—as long as they were made kosher, that is, fit to eat and permitted by Jewish law.

The German Jews who came to *Kleindeutschland* in the middle of the nineteenth century brought foods that became part of both Jewish and American cuisines. Isaac Gellis and others, arriving with sausage-making equipment, produced kosher hot dogs (vernacular for frankfurters), and introduced the cured, smoked, pickled, and spiced meats of Jewish delicatessen, such as corned beef, pastrami, salami, knockwurst, and even tongue.

The immigrant Jews in the 1882–1924 period were much poorer than their German American co-religionists. The staple source of animal protein for the poor Lower East Siders was herring, which was sold on the street from barrels and cost only a few pennies each. A schmaltz (soft, tender) herring was scraped, gutted, washed, and eaten raw with onion and bread. This was a typical immigrant lunch, along with a glass of tea. I can't remember eating lox (German lachs), probably because it was too expensive for us. On the other hand, homemade gefilte fish (boiled and chopped fish patties) was a Lower East Side staple.

Lower East Side foods and dishes that have nostalgic appeal for Jewish Americans include: kreplach (Jewish wonton); borscht (beet soup served hot in the winter and cold in the summer); and chicken soup (nicknamed Jewish penicillin). My mother made the latter most Friday evenings. In the afternoon she would give me a few pennies to buy "soup greens" (carrot tops and other greens from assorted vegetables) and a parsnip or two from the fruit-and-vegetable store. My mother's chicken soup was inedible as far as I was concerned. She boiled the chicken in the stock until the flesh fell away from the bones. The grease floated to the top. It tasted like dishwater. My sister and I had to gulp it down—it was sacrilegious not to—or we got no dessert (usually plain Jell-O, unless we had company, when canned peach slices were added). I made the soup potable by adding large dollops of ketchup, thus turning the watery chicken sweat—as I called it to make my mother angry—into tomato soup. In restaurants or other people's homes chicken soup came with knaidlach (tiny dumplings) or kreplach.

Dishes my mother made and I enjoyed included lokshen kugel (noodle pudding) baked with lots of raisins in a large, covered frying pan on a gas burner. She made a delicious, spicy red cabbage soup. Matzo brei (pieces of matzo soaked in egg and fried) was a Sunday-morning favorite. I liked my mother's lokshen und arbes (noodle and chickpeas) soup with burnt onion pieces. Her tzimmis, made from grated carrots and raisins, was good, as were her potato latkes (tiny pancakes) served with apple sauce. Mamaliga (cornmeal mush) was an acquired taste. Sometimes mother served us boiled flanken (a kosher cut of beef), which was awful, yet the same cut in a pot roast with potatoes and carrots was delicious.

Of course we had bagels, rye bread, and bialys, bought from the grocer or the baker. Matzos in my house were only eaten during Passover. We kids called matzos "stitched cardboard," but we could stand for hours outside the window of the Streit's matzo factory on Rivington Street and watch the machine deliver unending sheets of matzos into the arms of white-coated workers.

My father and his brothers loved to eat something that even the thought of made me gag. They called it schmaltz, but it had nothing to do with herring, except perhaps its smell. It was rendered chicken fat solidified to the consistency of butter and used as a spread on bread. Less awful but not high on my list of culinary delights was kishke (derma), an animal's intestine stuffed with fat, flour, and spices that is baked until brown, sliced, and eaten as a side dish.

On the whole, Lower East Siders seldom drank hard liquor except on special occasions—and then only the men imbibed. The same was generally true for wine, although it has a place in Friday-night worship and at Passover celebrations. The wine was made from Concord grapes and fortified with a great deal of sugar. Several companies produced it, most famously Manischewitz and Schapiro's. When I walked up to Rivington Street to see the matzo makers, the delicious smell of fermenting grapes wafted from the Schapiro winery located only a few doors down.

The immigrants and their offspring loved seltzer. Some may have believed the carbonated water came from health spas because seltzer had a reputation for being a health drink. A seltzer man delivered capped, high-pressure bottles to apartments on a weekly basis, taking the empties back with him. My father sold seltzer from the soda fountain in his stand. A glass of "two cents plain" held six ounces. An embellished seltzer drink at the stand was called an egg cream, although it had neither egg nor cream in it. Chocolate syrup and a little milk were fizzed in a glass, topped off with more seltzer. The price was five cents.

Pastry sweets were treats at my grandma's place and at our house. Grandma Anna was famous for her apple strudel, which was made with folds of dough so thin "you could read a newspaper through it." Mother tried to do it once or twice but failed. Only grandma knew the secret of great strudel and that secret died with her. Like good sports, my sister and I ate mom's strudel anyway. Occasionally we had store-bought schnecken (sticky buns), ruggelach (square-shaped pastries wrapped in dough and filled with raisins and nuts), and various kuchen (cakes) and hamantashen (a poppy seed pastry, usually filled with prunes or apricot jam, in the shape of a tricorn hat) at Purim. My mother really never took to baking. She eyed a gas oven warily. Her snack food was arbes, boiled chickpeas dried and seasoned with salt and pepper.

Street food from carts offered up treats costing only pennies. In the winter sweet potatoes were available from sheet-metal stoves on wheels, as were roasted chestnuts. Other stove carts sold sweet corn or dispensed apples and dried fruit dipped in hot jelly. In the summer fruit ices were sold on the street. Pretzels were available year-round. A confection called charlotte russe, consisting of whipped cream on plain cake, was eaten in cool weather.

When I was a child Delancey Street seemed to be a place filled with mythical, wonderful restaurants, although my favorite eating stop on the street was not even a restaurant. Levy's frankfurter shop on the corner of Essex Street sold a hot dog and a root beer in a mug for ten cents! The hot dog was not kosher, so my parents were not supposed to find out about my grazing trips north. Mom and dad were not fastidious in keeping a kosher kitchen at home, but they would have been upset if Orthodox Jewish customers had seen me eating trefe (unkosher food) and had reported the incident to them. In 1944, when we moved back to the Bronx, sliced ham and shrimp (both trefe) miraculously appeared in the refrigerator we now owned.

Ratner's kosher dairy restaurant was the most famous Delancey Street eatery. (Sadly, it closed in 2002, after almost one hundred years in business.) On a few occasions Uncle Artie, my father's policeman brother, would invite his brothers, sister, and their families to a communal dinner at Ratner's. I loved the little onion rolls in baskets best of all. The cheese blintzes and sour cream were a big hit too. Everyone kept an eye on Uncle Abie, who thought that everything on a restaurant table automatically became the property of the diner, including salt and pepper shakers, sugar bowls, and flatware. To facilitate his foraging, he brought a shopping bag that he placed strategically between his legs. It was hard to discourage him.

Delancey Street also had some kosher steak restaurants. A generous relative once took me to one called the French Romanian. In it I had an eating epiphany! I tasted a piece of steak I actually liked! On the few occasions mother broiled a piece of steak, she turned it into shoe leather by overcooking it. She was always afraid that she wouldn't "get the blood out." In the restaurant the steak was still slightly red, tender, and tasty.

Katz's Delicatessen on Houston Street was out of my walking range; my parents would not have taken me there because it was not kosher. I never had a knish (a potato- or kasha [buckwheat]-filled pastry) at Yonah Schimmel's on Houston Street, a century-old knish bakery, but knishes were widely available elsewhere on the Lower East Side.

Lower East Side food was never considered gourmet either at home or in the restaurants. However, food was very important since it reminded these strangers in the New World just who they were and where they had come from. When the new immigrants were poor and hungry, they realized that food was amazingly abundant in America, and that hard work, daily prayer, and a little mazel (luck) could allow them to eat as well and as much as they wanted. The slightly more affluent Jews became patrons of the Lower East Side's finer restaurants, reminding them of how far they had come. Thus, when the immigrants' children and grandchildren worked hard and had money to spend, they also ate well and in large quantities—perhaps even too much. And mostly they forgot the prayers.

The Lower East Side Tenement Museum on Orchard Street

In the last half of the nineteenth century thousands of five- to seven-story apartment buildings were constructed to house the flood of immigrants pouring into the Lower East Side and other parts of New York City. These apartments originally had no running water; later they had no hot water. In my childhood the Lower East Side was still filled with cold-water flats. After indoor toilets were introduced, they were shared by several families. Indeed, more than one family might live in one of the four flats on a floor, or, more commonly, a family would take in boarders to help pay the rent and to cover household expenses. Social reformers and the Yiddish press worked hard to improve the awful conditions under which tenement dwellers lived. Reform legislation in 1879 and 1901 eventually led to new constructions, with running water in each flat, more interior windows, and unobstructed fire escapes.

Under the auspices of the Lower East Side Tenement Museum (founded in 1988), one tenement at 97 Orchard Street, built in 1863 and first owned by a German tailor, has been restored and refurbished to re-create the life of immigrants at different periods in the history of this particular residence. This tenement sheltered thousands of people in its day. From 1870 to 1915 alone around ten thousand people lived in this one building, mostly immigrant German Jews and gentiles, Eastern European Jews, and Italians. It was boarded up from 1935 to 1987, and after necessary repairs it was opened to the public in 1994. The restoration, exhibiting as it does the hard life of the immigrant, is a testimony to the faith, strength, and determination of those who came to New York City with high hopes starting in the 1880s and continuing to this day. No wonder the museum has become a major tourist attraction for the descendants of immigrants who chose New York City as the gateway to America in the late nineteenth and early twentieth centuries.

Now, as part of the second Diaspora to the suburbs, they try to comprehend the struggle of their forebears, who made their first American home in a Lower East Side tenement like 97 Orchard Street, a residence with twenty-two apartments and two stores flanking a high entrance stoop that faced out on a street once thronged from morn to night with Yiddish-speaking people. Today it seems as exotic and as distant to us as a street in ancient Baghdad or Jerusalem.

The Lower East Side Tenement Museum has also created the first archive documenting the immigrant experience. The collective history of those urban workers and their families, the multitude of hope-driven newcomers who contributed so much to American culture and prosperity, is thus safely preserved for future scholars. In 1998 the federal government designated the Tenement Museum as an Affiliated Area of the National Park Service, linking it with such other landmarks of immigration to the Lower East Side as Castle Garden, Ellis Island, and, of course, the Statue of Liberty.

Moving On

New York City—perhaps all cities—is an image in flux. This moment represents only a few frames of stopped-motion, exposed film. Although there is still a small but vibrant Jewish community on the Lower East Side, most members are old. In time the last old Jew living on the Lower East Side will move or die. I used to think that person would be Uncle Abie, who at age ninety-four was still living alone in a flat overlooking the Brooklyn Bridge in the Alfred E. Smith projects on South Street, and who died just a few years ago. However, when I walk the streets of my old neighborhood I see there are some more.

Although much of the past remains, the area is rapidly changing. It is an old story in New York City: neighborhoods rise and fall and rise again. Old tenement buildings are being renovated and transformed into modern housing. Affluent younger people are moving there from the suburbs. A few gourmet restaurants and nightclubs have found the venue attractive and profitable. I still find it hard to imagine that in 2002 a Howard Johnson's Express Inn opened on Houston Street.

Yes, Katz's delicatessen, Guss's famous pickle stand (which recently moved from Essex to Orchard Street), and Yonah Schimmel's Knishes will close one day. The sellers of Jewish books and religious paraphernalia will disappear from Essex Street. The last synagogue will become an artist's studio. High-rise condos will grow tall where six-story tenements squatted for 150 years. Only the Yiddish letters spelling *Forverts* below the clock on the nationally registered Jewish Daily Forward Building will serve as the epitaph for a lost world— but ironically no one will be able to read it. Nevertheless, the words of such Lower East Side writers as Abraham Cahan, Anzia Yezierska, Michael Gold, Henry Roth, among others, will keep the memory of a powerful, vibrant, historically significant heritage alive.

Part Two

Early Jewish American Writers

The Writers

In the beginning Jewish writers living on, or having emerged from, the Lower East Side in the 1882–1924 period were immigrants or children of immigrants. English was not their first language. By choosing to write in the language of their adopted home they were attempting to reach out to a wider public. Indeed, writing in English was a part of their Americanization process. They prided themselves on mastering a language with an enormous number of readers. They succeeded in stepping onto a global stage. But they were still Jews—specifically Lower East Side Jews—even when they tried to disguise that truth through religious conversion or marriage to a non-Jew. Like Irish writers in the twentieth century and today, they were writing for their home population and the worldwide English-speaking community at the same time. Which audience was primary and which secondary was an individual matter for these early Jewish American writers.

The first generation of Jewish American authors started the tradition of both erudite and popular writing. They left a legacy for all Americans—one that now includes the works of Saul Bellow, Paddy Chayefsky, Edward Dahlberg, Babette Deutsch, E. L. Doctorow, Kenneth Fearing, Edna Ferber, Bruce Jay Friedman, Allen Ginsburg, Anthony Hecht, Joseph Heller, Lillian Hellman, Fannie Hurst, David Ignatow, George S. Kaufman, Maxine Kumin, Stanley Kunitz, Tony Kushner, Denise Levertov, Meyer Levin, David Mamet, Norman Mailer, Bernard Malamud, Arthur Miller, Howard Nemerov, Clifford Odets, Tillie Olsen, Cynthia Ozick, Grace Paley, Dorothy

Parker, Marge Piercy, Robert Pinsky, Chaim Potok, Elmer Rice, Adrienne Rich, Philip Roth, J. D. Salinger, Budd Schulberg, Karl Shapiro, Irwin Shaw, Neil Simon, Susan Sontag, Gertrude Stein, Leon Uris, Wendy Wasserstein, Nathanael West, Herman Wouk, and many others. It seems obvious that Jewish American culture is partly a literary manifestation that began in a unique neighborhood. Happily that culture lives on and flourishes.

Antecedents in American Literature

It was inevitable that the vibrant ghetto culture would expand and produce high-quality writing that would catch the attention of the American public, many of whose readers were very interested in the ethos, values, and lifestyles of these new immigrants who seemed so ambitious, so anxious to experience life, and so filled with energy and drive. Those Americans predisposed to anti-Semitism found in the new Jewish American literature confirmation of negative stereotypes. Indeed, some parent-hating or self-hating Jewish American writers of the second or third generation who were now living the American dream consciously reinforced negative stereotypes through satire and a selective realism. For the most part, however, such bigotry was a phenomenon tied to the Depression and the 1940s, years of a general and strident anti-Semitism in the United States and Europe. Almost without exception the first generation of Jewish American writers simply presented realistic, warts-and-all portrayals of their fellow immigrants or their parents' generation.

Themes

The first generation of Lower East Side writers encompassed many themes in their work, some resulting from the experience of immigration and acculturation, others from the household tensions brought about by relocation, poverty, generational conflict, "smother" love, and patriarchal tyranny. Trying to comprehend, cope with, and accept the merciless capitalistic system into which all immigrants were thrust is a recurring theme. The Lower East Side workplace was a compactor of workers, mashing former yeshiva students, educated *gymnasium* graduates, Talmudic sages, homemakers, and unskilled children into a sausage machine that ground out garments, artificial flowers, and cigars. The newly created urban proletariat was shocked to discover that their unfeeling employers were often co-religionists—German Jews whose grandparents had been immigrants in the same neighborhood the Eastern European Jews now inhabited. Alternatively, the new capitalists might be recent Eastern European Jews or their children who may have had a little capital to start with or, more likely, had caught on quickly to the exploitive system.

The writers also addressed the question of assimilation, some seeing it as a mixed blessing, others as an unfortunate consequence of coming to America. But when the ultimate results of assimilation are self-hatred and intermarriage, it is always a family tragedy. Among virtually all the Jewish American writers of the mass-immigration period there is a sense that their religion is dying. It slowly vanishes from the texts. The Orthodox Jewish practices of Eastern Europe not only do not mesh with those of the New World but seem to make the individual unfit for that world.

Significantly, although anti-Semitism is a theme in the early texts, it is seldom a major one. This seeming deemphasis did not mean that it was not present in the immigration and post-immigration experience of Lower East Side Jews but rather that the Eastern European Jews had always lived with it and expected outbreaks of it. Though anti-Semitism had no legal status and was not accompanied by bloody pogroms, racism and class discrimination was part of the American way of life at the turn of the twentieth century.

Early Jewish American fiction is built around a series of quests, either symbolic or practical, not the least of which is the desire for physical comfort and material success, which, when achieved, is usually accompanied by guilt feelings toward friends and family left behind, as well as a sense of betrayal of the spiritual and humane precepts of Judaism.

Another archetypal quest is what may be called the Telemachus theme: searching for and finding the lost father. For the young members or children of the immigrant generation the Jewish father symbolized the controlling religion from which they wished and strove to escape. As mature adults, however, they felt both guilt over their seeming betrayal and a deep sense of loss of a moral center. Lastly, the Lower East Side writers struggled for recognition and acceptance from the mainstream American world of letters as well as the general reading public. Individually their work was often cathartic, an outlet for repressed feelings about parents, siblings, unattainable mates, lack of acceptance, and other insecurities. Leaving self-analytic investigation and self-justification aside, they were above all literary artists.

City Fiction

The Jewish world below Fourteenth Street began to interest the American reading public even before the first Jewish American writers began to recount their immigrant experience in English. Partly because of the influence of sensational journalism in the last half of the nineteenth century, the American public began to think of the Lower East Side as an exotic, dangerous, lawless, erotic, and intriguing foreign enclave. The streets were presented as full of prostitutes. Drugs were thought to be readily available and in frequent use. Fagin-like fences sold stolen goods openly. One might be mugged, or a woman could be doped and sold into "white slavery." Readers wanted to go "slumming" vicariously. *The Nether Side of New York: or, The Vice, Crime, and Poverty of the Great Metropolis* (1872) by Edward Crapsey, the brother of poet Adelaïde Crapsey, and Charles Loring Brace's *The Dangerous Classes of New York, and Twenty Years' Work Among Them* (1872) are just two examples of books that fueled a voyeuristic and sometimes prurient interest.

A truer picture of Lower East Side life was presented in Jacob A. Riis's *How the Other Half Lives* (1890). Major American writers of realistic fiction began to show interest in the Lower East Side, reflected in such works as William Dean Howells's novel *A Hazard of New Fortunes* (1890). Howells capitalized on the growing interest in the "foreign" neighborhoods of New York City and is credited with founding a subdivision of late-nineteenth- and early-twentieth-century writing called city fiction. Other well-known writers who contributed to this subgenre include Brander Matthews, Edward

Townsend, and Richard Harding Davis, the most famous journalist of his time. Even more important are Stephen Crane's Bowery novels: *Maggie, A Girl of the Streets* (1893) and *George's Mother* (1896). Theodore Dreiser also sets part of *Sister Carrie* (1900) on the Bowery. With these latter novels the notorious Bowery—the haunt of criminals, drug addicts, derelicts, and prostitutes—is presented as a microcosm of the Lower East Side, something it assuredly was not.

At the turn of the twentieth century Abraham Cahan, writing in English, began to publish immigrant novels set on the Lower East Side, signaling the birth of Jewish American literature. It should be noted that several writers—taking a cue from Cahan—later memorialized other immigrant communities. Although born on the Lower East Side, Daniel Fuchs grew up in Brooklyn. In *The Williamsburg Trilogy* (*Summer in Williamsburg* [1934], *Homage to Blenholt* [1936], *Low Company* [1937]), the novelist chronicled immigrant life across the Williamsburg Bridge. It was a life not very different from immigrant life on the Lower East Side, but the place lacked the culture, the social and political ferment, and the local color of the latter. In his 1937 novel *The Old Bunch* Meyer Levin described the second-generation Jewish American experience on Chicago's West Side. In his Studs Lonigan trilogy—especially the first novel entitled *Young Lonigan* (1932)—James T. Farrell depicted Irish American tenement life on the South Side of Chicago. Farrell was performing the same task for and about the children of Irish immigrants as Anzia Yezierska, Michael Gold, and Henry Roth were doing for the children of Eastern European Jewish immigrants.

Abraham Cahan
1860–1951

When in 1896 D. Appleton and Company of New York published Abraham Cahan's short novel *Yekl, a Tale of the New York Ghetto,* it opened a path for Jewish American literature. William Dean Howells, the chief preceptor of American literature at the time—and Cahan's mentor—hailed the latter as a new master of literary realism. But writing fiction in English was only a small part of Cahan's long career. He was a great socialist leader of East Side Jewry, the major spokesperson for the American Jewish community, and the founder and for decades the editor-in-chief of the *Jewish Daily Forward,* the most important Yiddish-language newspaper in America.

Abraham Cahan was born in Podberezy, near Vilna, Lithuania, which was then within the Russian Empire. When he was five years old his Orthodox Jewish family moved to Vilna (now Vilnius), where a large intellectual and politically active Jewish population thrived and where his parents hoped Abraham would eventually be ordained as a rabbi. But Cahan's basic education was Russian. From 1877 to 1881 he studied at the Teachers' Institute in Vilna and was certified to teach in Jewish schools where Russian was the language of instruction. He soon became active in radical socialist politics, fleeing to escape prosecution after the assassination of Czar Alexander II in 1881, an event that was immediately followed by widespread government-sponsored pogroms.

Cahan arrived in New York City in 1882 without money and in need of work. Like tens of thousands of unskilled Jews, he found employment in the cigar factories. He hastened to learn the language of his new country. In a year he began publishing newspaper articles in English. His first article, an 1883 piece in the *New York World,* attacked imperial Russia. An ardent socialist, Cahan championed labor and helped organize several unions.

Cahan was a humanist and an atheist. He loved the Jewish people, and he strove to show the world how rich Jewish culture was, and how much the Jewish people shared the hopes and aspirations, the needs and the gifts, the compassion and the love of life, of all humanity.

In 1897 Cahan helped found the Yiddish-language *Jewish Daily Forward.* Initially it floundered and Cahan left it, only to return in 1903 as its editor, spearheading its successful drive to become the leading Jewish newspaper in America and a mighty voice for American Jewry. At the height of its popularity the *Forward* had a daily readership numbering 250,000. Cahan made sure that the newspaper devoted much of its space to the arts. He was responsible for introducing the fiction of Nobel Prize–winning author Isaac Bashevis Singer, Israel Joshua Singer (Isaac's older brother), and Sholem Asch to the Yiddish-reading public. Cahan's socialism never deteriorated into communism. Initially welcoming the Russian Revolution in 1917, by 1921 Cahan realized that the revolution had been diverted from true socialism and that Bolshevism presented as despotic a threat to democracy as had Russian imperialism.

Cahan's wife, Anna Bronstein Cahan, a well-educated intellectual from Kiev whom he had married in 1886, encouraged him to write fiction. His first published story, "A Providential Match," was written in Yiddish. Later he translated it into English and it was collected in *The Imported Bridegroom and Other Stories of the New York Ghetto* (1898). This collection followed the nascent work of Jewish American fiction *Yekl, a Tale of the New York Ghetto* (1896), which was turned into the popular film *Hester Street* (1974) by the director Joan Micklin Silver.

The two great influences on Cahan's fiction were the naturalism of American writers like Stephen Crane, Upton Sinclair, Ernest Poole, and Frank Norris, as well as the European naturalism of Émile Zola, Israel Zangwill, and especially Maxim Gorky. Like each of these writers, Cahan exposed a segment of humanity and a way of life few readers knew anything about. A basic idea behind naturalism was to change the perception of urban existence in the minds of middle- and upper-class readers.

With *Yekl, a Tale of the New York Ghetto* Cahan, himself an immigrant, depicted the immigrant experience almost as if he were a reporter. For the first time the American reading public could see the life of these brand-new Americans through the eyes of a knowledgeable and sympathetic insider.

Yekl is Jake Podgorny, a young Jewish immigrant with a wife, Gitl, and son, Yoselé, waiting in Russia to be sent for by him. When the story opens, he has been living in the United States for three years. Since Yekl, a Yiddish nickname for the Hebrew Ya'Kov (Jacob), was what he was called in Russia, it may be assumed that he has given himself an Anglicized version—Jake—as part of his Americanization. In Russia Jake lived in a shtetl and worked as a blacksmith in his father's shop. His Jewish education was very limited and he is basically illiterate. After marriage and the birth of Yoselé, Jake left for America to improve his economic condition. He was able to find work in the garment industry on the Lower East Side of New York City, having earlier worked in a sweatshop in Boston. He doesn't seem to miss his wife and child. Jake Podgorny is undergoing an identity crisis. He wants to believe that he is no longer a greenhorn even though he speaks English with a thick Yiddish accent. He behaves arrogantly toward his fellow workers, believing they are less Americanized than himself. Conversely, they see him as pretentious and boorish. Jake has one friend at work, Bernstein, a learned and religious man.

Jake does not reveal that he is married with a son back home because he enjoys going to a dancing academy, where he is popular and can embrace "American" girls, who, in reality, are immigrant women who have lived in the city for a few years more than Jake. One young woman in particular, Mamie, an attractive blond originally from Poland, has caught his fancy.

One day Jake receives a letter revealing that his father has died. He is filled with remorse and sends for Gitl and Yoselé. In order to do this, he borrows some money from Mamie, who assumes that their relationship will lead to marriage. When Jake and Gitl meet again, they hardly recognize each other. He is clean-shaven and dressed the way a nobleman dressed in the old country. On the other hand, Gitl shocks Jake with the wig she must wear as a married Orthodox Jewish woman. Moreover, her shtetl clothes make it obvious that she is a greenhorn. The Podgonys set up a household in an apartment, with Jake's friend Bernstein as a boarder to help pay the rent. Jake tries to be a good father and to adjust to his disappointing wife, while Gitl tries to Americanize herself a little in a futile attempt to please her husband.

Mamie, having learned that Jake is married and has a son, reappears and demands her money. Jake now longs for Mamie. He asks her for more money to help him escape from his marriage. Mamie confesses that she loves him and Jake realizes that he loves her. They agree that he will divorce his wife so they can marry. At the Jewish divorce proceedings, which take place in a rabbi's apartment, Gitl, though visibly upset, appears to have metamorphosed into a well-dressed American woman. Now she and Bernstein, who has cared for Gitl and her son from the moment he saw them, will marry and buy a grocery store with the proceeds from the divorce settlement. Jake and Mamie head for City Hall to be married in a civil ceremony. Jake feels that he has somehow been defeated. He is not ready to give up his brief freedom. The irony is potent. As the saying goes, he has jumped out of the frying pan into the fire. Materialistic Mamie will be hard to live with.

In *Yekl,* as elsewhere, Cahan is not only a realist but a moralist. Although Jake has our sympathy at the end of the tale, the reader simultaneously feels that Gitl has found justice after all. Poor Jake did not really understand the new culture he embraced so wholeheartedly, nor did he understand the value of the culture he abandoned with the jettisoning of his loving wife and son.

Two years after *Yekl* Cahan published a collection of five short stories in *The Imported Bridegroom* (1898). Two of the stories first appeared, in different versions, in the magazine *Short Story* in 1895. "A Providential Match" is a tale of clashing cultures. In the old country Rouvke was a poor young man who drove a wagon for a distiller. He admired the distiller's daughter, Hanele, but she was far above his station. In the New World he quickly becomes an "American" in appearance if not in speech and earns a comfortable living dealing in anything he can get his hands on. Still, he has not found a woman willing to marry him; this is partly because he is physically unattractive. A marriage broker informs him that the distiller has fallen on hard times and a match with Hanele—who is now at the "advanced" age of twenty-five—is a possibility. Rouvke hesitates, calculating that if he could marry the daughter of an East Side merchant with a dowry, he could do even better in business. But pride and passion win out over good business sense. Hanele's father, initially outraged at Rouvke's seeking his daughter, finally consents. Rouvke sends money for her passage and to purchase new clothes.

When she disembarks at the Castle Garden immigrant arrival center, the beautiful Hanele comes ashore arm in arm with a young college student. They have had a shipboard romance and wish to remain together. Rouvke loudly demands the return of his money, but a burley hustler for an immigrant hotel motions to the couple to follow him while shoving Rouvke aside. Left without bride or money, he is the laughingstock of the friends he brought along to witness his success in romance. In the end, the reader has sympathy for the lonely immigrant. He has learned a painful lesson: new clothes and cash in hand do not make an uneducated, uncouth, and greedy man handsome and desirable. Cahan's antimaterialistic message transcends the world of the Lower East Side.

"A Sweat-Shop Romance" is set in a tenement flat. A husband, wife, and four other workers are employed in a small business. A female worker, Beile the finisher, is quietly admired by Heyman, who operates the sewing machine. She is fond of him too, but he does not know it. The wife of the shop owner wrongly tries to use Beile as her servant. The presser, David, knows this is wrong and advises Beile to refuse to run an errand for the wife. The latter vents her fury, and Beile and David quit. The meek Heyman, meanwhile, has sat silently. It takes him two weeks to get up the nerve to go to Beile's tenement in order to tell her that he is sorry for the trouble she experienced, but he is too late. He hears Beile and David's betrothal celebration in progress. "A Sweat-Shop Romance" is slight. The plot is too sentimental, but the depiction of the often desperate sweatshop life is more realistic than most such depictions at that time. When Cahan demonstrated his affiliation with naturalism, he proved his skill as a creative writer.

The title story of *The Imported Bridegroom,* like *Yekl,* is a minor masterpiece. In it Cahan introduces a main theme in his fiction, one that undergirds *The Rise of David Levinsky,* namely, that material success, even in America, does not necessarily spell true success. Material success may lead to personal failure and emotional unhappiness. As the old saying goes, "Money can't buy happiness."

The central character of "The Imported Bridegroom" is Asriel Stroom, a successful, retired fifty-eight-year-old Lower East Side businessman, now a widower. Stroom, an Orthodox Jew, is growing more religious by the day and is waxing nostalgic for his old shtetl community of Pravly, in Poland. Thirty-five years earlier he had departed, a poor, insignificant youth. Now the shtetl has grown beautiful and idyllic in his memory. Stroom lives in his house on Mott Street with his young daughter, Flora, whom he loves dearly and whom he has spoiled more than a little. Flora is of marriageable age, and Stroom would like to match her up with a successful and religious businessman.

Flora, however, has ideas of her own. She has some education. She plays the piano. She has a library and reads the great Victorian novels. Although she is proud of her command of English, it in fact leaves something to be desired. In reality, Flora is a trifle vulgar. She has no intention, however, of marrying an uncouth parvenu, someone very much like her father, even though she truly loves him. Her mind is set on marrying a Jewish doctor and living uptown.

Stroom returns to Pravly for a visit and amuses himself, especially when he reflects on the fact that he is wealthy enough to buy and sell the whole village. Stroom enjoys going to the services in the old synagogue. There, however, he comes into conflict with Pravly's leading citizen, Reb Lippe. Offering a large gift to the synagogue for the privilege of reading the *sedra,* the weekly portion of the Torah, Stroom is countered by the jealous Lippe; although Stroom wins the bidding war, he is cheated out of the honor.

Stroom is furious. The rich, prideful man has religious conviction but not humility. Once more the leaders of the shtetl have made him feel inferior. He gets his revenge on Reb Lippe by besting him in a dowry auction for a religious son-in-law, Shaya, a Talmudic prodigy, who was to marry Lippe's daughter. Triumphant, Stroom takes his "imported bridegroom" to New York City, dresses him in American clothes, and presents him to Flora, who is shocked and horrified. She will not be matched to a greenhorn, and she will not even think about marrying Shaya.

Stroom, however, is clever in the ways of a man and a maid. He does not push Flora, but rather has Shaya stay in the house, receiving English lessons from Flora as well as an outside teacher paid for by Stroom. Soon Flora is very interested in the young, pleasant-featured, and obviously brilliant housemate. Shaya quickly comes to care for Flora too. Shaya has also found the Astor Library, where he feasts on forbidden secular knowledge. Now the determined girl will have her cake and eat it too—or so she thinks. She plots against her father. Shaya will go to college, study medicine, and become her Jewish doctor-husband. Shaya is willing. They tell Stroom that they are betrothed, and he and Tamara, the elderly housekeeper, are delighted. They don't tell the older people of their conspiracy. It seems to Stroom that his fondest dreams will come true. He will have a prestigious son-in-law who will say prayers for his soul after he has died.

To his horror, Stroom learns that Shaya has been seen going into the library and even smoking on the Sabbath. When he follows Shaya one day and sees him entering a nonkosher restaurant, he is shaken and angered. Shaya is confronted and banished, but Flora runs after him. They rush to City Hall for a civil marriage ceremony. Stroom is willing to forgive them and he arranges an Orthodox marriage, but he has lost his taste for life in "godless" America, so he proposes marriage to Tamara and immigration to the Holy Land after Flora and Shaya complete their ceremony.

In true O. Henry fashion, Flora, triumphant, runs to get Shaya to meet with her father. Shaya is pleased that his benefactor will reconcile with him, but he asks Flora to make a detour with him, taking her to a smoke-filled room where his English teacher and other intellectuals are engaged in a heated philosophical debate. Shaya has applied his Talmudic hermeneutic skills to secular philosophy. Flora is completely left out. She is stunned and desolate. She realizes that she will not be married to a doctor but to a poor intellectual who will treat her only as an appendage to his life as a scholar. She might as well have married a rabbi.

Again the irony is brilliant. The imported bridegroom is happy, as he should be, given his innocence. But Flora's plot has boomeranged, and Stroom's arrogance has brought him great disappointment. The moral seems to be: "Man plans and God laughs." Another outstanding aspect of "The Imported Bridegroom" is its contrasting evocation of life on the Lower East Side and life in a Polish shtetl. Shaya, Flora, and Stroom are, moreover, strong, vivid characters.

"Circumstances" was first published in *Cosmopolitan* (22 April 1897). The story depicts how life in New York City at the end of the nineteenth century was destructive of married life for those whose new existence required hard manual labor for which they were untrained and unprepared.

An intellectual Russian Jewish couple, Tanya and Boris, are struggling on the Lower East Side. They left Russia when Boris learned that he would have to convert to Christianity in order to become a lawyer. Now he slaves in a button factory. They grow desperate for money in the slack season and take in a boarder, Dalsky, who is Boris's friend and former schoolmate. Unfortunately, Tanya falls is love with Dalsky, who leaves in order to ease the situation. Tanya, however, is so in love with Dalsky that she can no longer live with her husband. She finds a place to live by herself and learns to operate a sewing machine in a sweatshop. Both Boris and Tanya are now unhappy and lonely.

In "Circumstances" Cahan seems to be saying that the struggle for survival in America may be worse than the life of limited freedom and anti-Semitism in czarist Russia. There, at least, there was respect for intellectual and cultured people even if they were Jewish. In New York City all immigrants were transformed into interchangeable proletarians slaving for subsistence wages.

"A Ghetto Wedding" was first published in *The Atlantic* (February 1898). It is a sentimental story reminiscent of an O. Henry short story. A young couple who are both garment industry workers, Goldie and Nathan, wish to marry, but the bride-to-be insists upon waiting until they can afford an expensive and elaborate affair with two hundred guests. A slack season reduces her expectations as Nathan, now out of work, has had to turn peddler, but she is still determined to have a large wedding, greedily calculating that it would pay for itself with the gifts received, and that they would also be given expensive furnishings for an apartment. They "invest" all their cash to cover a feast for 150 guests. Alas, times are so hard that only twenty guests appear and the gifts are inconsequential.

At the dismal wedding dinner Goldie realizes her folly. To make matters worse, while walking home to their small flat—Goldie, who had insisted they arrive at the wedding in a carriage, refuses to spend money on a ride home—the couple is taunted by an anti-Semitic gang hanging out in front of a saloon. With the danger past, they realize that what happened that evening was insignificant, and that they were beginning to experience the happiness they had longed for. As in all the early stories, Cahan is skillful in creating character and setting a ghetto scene. But the obvious plot of "A Ghetto Wedding" is sentimentalized to the point where it loses its credibility as a believable portrait of ghetto life.

Between 1899 and 1901 Cahan published six more stories in *Cosmopolitan, Scribner's, Century,* and *The Atlantic Monthly* that have not yet been collected. In 1905 he published *The White Terror and the Red,* a novel about revolutionary activity in Russia prior to the assassination of Czar Alexander II, the event that triggered the massive pogroms that provoked hundreds of thousands of Eastern European Jews to abandon their ancestral homes for America. The story involves the relationship of Prince Pavel Boulatoff and his Jewish lover, Clara Yavna. Pavel becomes a nihilist. He wants to marry Clara but she fears that eventually they would be caught and killed. The little time they have must be devoted to the revolutionary cause. A plot to kill the czar is successful, but it is followed by widespread pogroms. The despairing couple marry, are captured, and are awaiting death in prison as the novel ends.

Although Cahan knew his subject well, *The White Terror and the Red* is not a successful novel. It is marred by Cahan's attempt to teach history as well as write fiction. Characters embrace the revolutionary cause with little apparent motivation. It is also marred by a melodramatic streak, for when the opportunity to escape capture and death by fleeing to America arises, they don't take it. Fortunately, Cahan was not entirely discouraged. He now had the experience of writing a long and involved narrative, one that served him well in his last and greatest effort to write fiction in English.

The publication history of *The Rise of David Levinsky* began in 1913 with its four-part serialization in *McClure's Magazine.* The intent was to show how a Jewish immigrant might rise from abject poverty to great wealth. The key was success in the garment industry. Immediately upon arriving on the Lower East Side, immigrant Jews from Eastern Europe entered the ready-made clothing manufacturing industry in large numbers. The industry had largely been controlled by German American Jews who had resided in the New World for one or two generations. Newer immigrants quickly set up competing factories and drove their co-religionists out of much of the trade, especially women's apparel.

In *The Rise of David Levinsky* Cahan was not only writing fiction but was recording a chapter in American economic history. Cahan was never in love with money. It was therefore easy for him to show how the capitalistic pursuit of wealth by individuals was morally debasing and detrimental to happiness. This is what Cahan's mentor William Dean Howells had claimed in his famous novel *The Rise of Silas Lapham* (1885), the work that strongly influenced Cahan. Paradoxically, the unsentimental Cahan knew that developing industries could and would lead to better wages and a higher standard of living for workers. But he also realized the latter needed the support and guidance of unions in order to achieve economic justice.

Collective good did emerge from individual greed, as the Scottish political economist Adam Smith had predicted in his *Wealth of Nations* (1776), but not by letting that greed run rampant without social restraints. I suppose Cahan intuitively understood American business, capital formation, and the accumulation of power better than most social scientists and critics of his time. And he was not scornful of enterprise.

As a well-educated new American Cahan could view the contemporary scene both as a Jewish immigrant and as a member of the American establishment. He could read both the dominant culture and the subculture for which he served as mediator as well as translator. He could see and point up the shortcomings of some of his co-religionists while simultaneously valorizing the collective achievement of entrepreneurial Eastern European Jewish immigrants, who pursued the American dream of material success and made it their own. Still, it took a long time for Cahan's readers, both Jew and gentile, to appreciate his truthful analysis of Jewish drive. Some felt that by depicting individual Jews engaged in unprincipled business practices Cahan was reinforcing negative stereotypes and evidencing a degree of Jewish self-hatred. The charge was and remains unfair. David Levinsky is a true-to-life character. He is as much to be pitied as he is to be disliked.

The final version of *The Rise of David Levinsky* (1917), Cahan's last work of fiction, quickly became the first classic of Jewish American literature. It is also a major work of early-twentieth-century American social realism. To give him his due, Cahan's realism differs from the rest of the genre in that it is devoid of sensationalism and violence.

David Levinsky, the protagonist, is the person Cahan might have become if he had continued his Jewish education in Vilna and then emigrated to the United States. Though he was writing from a Russian socialist perspective, he infused the character of the rising industrialist with his own fascination with all things American. Unlike Anzia Yezierska, Michael Gold, or Henry Roth, Cahan imparts absolutely no Yiddish flavor or tone to his narrative. There is no attempt made to imitate a certain dialect; Cahan respects English and he respects the immigrant. Furthermore, it seems apparent that the ideal reader Cahan had in mind was the American-born gentile, who, as he correctly assumed, had the power to make life easier for the Jewish immigrants on the Lower East Side and would do so if the intelligence, humanity, and dignity of these fellow human beings were recognized. Thus, Cahan's characters speak English clearly and well, making the text easily accessible.

Cahan saw a kind of tragedy in the pursuit of wealth. Levinsky and, by extension, the nouveaux riches fell as easily as they had risen. The Faustian bargain was to tender one's soul in exchange for youth. Levinsky did it for wealth. The constant attention to making ever more money, the loss of friendships on the way up, the jettisoning of religion, the betrayal of comrades and loved ones, and the fading interest in things cultural slowly erode character. In the sense that Cahan's novel is about "making it," it is an American book. In the sense that it is about the exploitation of workers and the selfish manipulation of the means of production, it is a Russian socialist work.

In the sense that it is about the waste of an intelligent person and the loss of a soul, it is a Jewish tale.

The Rise of David Levinsky is told as a long flashback. The year is 1913 and Levinsky, a millionaire clothing manufacturer, is fifty-two years old—interestingly, about the same age as Cahan when he began to tell the story of David Levinsky. Cahan employs first-person narrative as Levinsky relates the events of his life up to the present. The writing reflects the plain American style of William Dean Howells and his contemporaries.

The lengthy novel is divided into fourteen books. The first four are set in the town of Antomir, in Russia. David's father died before the child was three years old and he and his impoverished, overprotective, Orthodox Jewish mother live in a corner of a cellar. She scrapes together funds to permit David to receive an Orthodox Jewish education. In a Talmudic seminary he befriends Naphtali, a gentle youth who eventually confesses that he does not believe in God. Mrs. Levinsky is proud that her son is a good student, but David's mind is not always on his studies. He thinks of women and he dwells on his hatred for a competing scholar. One day David returns home after having been beaten and harassed by gentiles. His fearless mother rushes out to attack his tormentors. Struck in the head, she is carried home and soon dies.

David is now hungry and penniless. A pious rich woman gives him meals regularly, but David has lost interest in his studies. He contemplates emigrating to America. But then he meets Matilda, the attractive "modern" daughter of the rich woman. She teases the Yeshiva boy and urges him to obtain a real education. David falls in love. They hug and kiss a lot and Matilda is willing to introduce him to sex, but he is so naïve that he fails to understand when she signals her receptivity. Matilda quickly tires of immature David but generously offers to obtain money for his passage to America. Although he is broken-hearted and would like to stay with her, he accepts the offer.

In books five through eight Cahan delineates, through Levinsky's first experiences in New York City, the struggles of a friendless Jewish immigrant who has no marketable skills, cannot speak English, and lacks relatives or friends in the city. Fortunately, a kind man he meets in a synagogue helps Levinsky, but his religion quickly leaves him. He becomes a peddler. Needing sexual relief, he frequents prostitutes. Homesick, he also longs for Matilda. Studying English in night school, he makes friends with his teacher, a Mr. Bender, who eventually will become one of Levinsky's loyal employees.

Instead of devoting himself entirely to peddling, in order to educate himself Levinsky becomes an avid reader of English novels by Dickens and his contemporaries (like Flora in "The Imported Bridegroom"). A chance East Side meeting with Gittleson, a tailor he first met aboard the immigrant ship, sends Levinsky into the garment industry as an apprentice sewing-machine operator, even though his real wish is to study at City College. At work he meets and proposes marriage to Gussie, a fellow worker, hoping that she will support him while he attends college, but she refuses to be exploited.

Having been humiliated at work by an overbearing boss, Levinsky determines to go into business for himself. Thoughts of higher education fly out the window. Levinsky charms the distrustful wife of a clothing designer named Chaikin. Scraping together capital and credit by whatever means possible, they start up their business, but it almost immediately fails due to bad luck.

In the ninth book David falls in love for the second time. Max Margolis, a friend, invites him home to meet his wife, Dora, and his young daughter, Lucy. Meanwhile, another friend lends him money and an unexpected check for goods arrives. Levinsky has his second chance. He becomes a boarder in the Margolis household, and he and Dora fall in love and have a brief affair. The young mother is guilt-ridden. Levinsky urges her to divorce her husband and marry him, but for the sake of her child Dora refuses and David moves out.

Although Levinsky is deeply saddened, business is booming. He has nonunion workers earning less than union scale and that gives him an advantage over the union shops. He has become the same kind of boss he once hated. Now he reads Charles Darwin and Herbert Spencer, the social Darwinist. Levinsky is convinced that he is succeeding because he is one of the "fittest," who always come out on top.

In the tenth book the reader learns of Levinsky's triumph as a manufacturer and his growing belief that he needs, indeed, deserves a wife. In the eleventh through thirteenth books Levinsky's personal and social life are emphasized. Matilda, now married to a Russian, has come to New York to lecture at the Great Hall in Cooper Union on behalf of radical prisoners in Russia. When Levinsky goes to the hall to meet her, she sees only an overdressed capitalist and spurns him. He, in turn, becomes truly reactionary, hardening his heart against workers and radicals alike.

At the age of forty Levinsky courts and proposes marriage to Fanny, the daughter of a rich businessman who is also a Talmudist. Although Levinsky is not in love with Fanny, he believes she would make an appropriate wife for him. Just before the marriage, he stops off at a Catskills resort, where he sees and falls head-over-heels in love with Anna Tevkin, the daughter of a Hebrew poet whose published love letters to his wife once sexually aroused David and his friend Naphtali in Antomir. Alas, Anna does not care for him at all. Nevertheless, he breaks his engagement and pursues Anna by courting her father, now a real estate broker in New York City, and inveigling himself into the interesting artistic and radical Tevkin family. When he finally asks Anna to marry him, she emphatically turns him down. Levinsky is devastated. He has lost the greatest love of his life.

The fourteenth book has Levinsky turning all his attention to business. His fortune multiplies. He meets Matilda again, and this time they are cordial toward each other. He tries to renew his friendship with Gitelson, but they are too far apart economically and socially to become long-term companions. Meeting old friends and flames only increases Levinsky's loneliness. He comes close to marrying an intelligent and kind gentile widow, but in sizing up the situation he realizes that the cultural gulf between them is too great. Moreover, when he begins to hint at a lasting relationship, she remains noncommittal.

So in the end David Levinsky finds some solace in reading great literature. If he can't live life in the flesh, he will live it in his imagination. He remains uneasy concerning his great wealth and feels the pull of his early upbringing and the memory of the poverty of his youth. All he can do is make money.

For Cahan plot evolves from character, and character is determined by environment. The environments of Levinsky's early life—a Russian town rife with poverty and anti-Semitism and the Lower

East Side at its most crowded and competitive—explain the barbed nature of his personality. Levinsky is not a likable protagonist. He let his widowed mother fight his battle for him and she was killed in the process. He uses her sacrifice to obtain sympathy and advantages from those who feel sorry for an orphan. In America he tries hard to fit in yet never quite succeeds. He has the clothes but not the class. He has abandoned education and culture in pursuit of money. He abandons his religion. He exploits people and discards them when they are no longer useful. His business practices, personifying social Darwinism, are excessively aggressive and sometimes border on the treacherous. He exploits his workers. He is disloyal. He betrays a friend by making love to the man's wife. Generally, he is manipulative with women. His egoism is off-putting and he is excessively self-satisfied.

Yet the reader also feels sorry for this melancholy, alienated, deracinated immigrant. Although beaten down as a child and youth, Levinsky cannot admit to himself the fact that he is always a little frightened and unsure beneath his sneering pose of intellectual superiority and great wealth. It's a cliché, of course, but Levinsky never learns that happiness can't really be bought. He will never be happy or content.

Late-nineteenth- and early-twentieth-century Jewish New York is also a character in this realist novel. The overcrowded flats; the restless, teeming streets; the soul-destroying sweatshops; the nascent Yiddish theater; the synagogues; the cafés with their poets and intellectuals—all figure in Cahan's vision. The vastness of the metropolis makes its inhabitants painfully aware that they are even more distant from each other than they would be in a less populated environment. Consequently, implies Cahan the moralist, people must strive to be more caring and responsible toward each other.

Other environments also contribute to characterization. Antomir, the Russian village of Levinsky's birth, is a reification of Eastern European Jewish life. The marriage market at the Catskills summer resort shows how crass young women and fortune-seeking young men attempt to best each other. There young women are peddled on their looks and their fathers' money—not necessarily in that order.

In *The Rise of David Levinsky* Abraham Cahan created one of the greatest characters in Jewish American fiction. David Levinsky may not be a titan of industry, but he is a titan of the late-nineteenth- and early-twentieth-century school of American literary realism.

Additional Reading

Cahan, Abraham. *The Education of Abraham Cahan* (autobiography). Philadelphia: Jewish Publication Society of America, 1969.
———. *The Rise of David Levinsky.* New York: Penguin, 1993.
———. *"Yekl" and "The Imported Bridegroom" and Other Stories of Yiddish New York.* Reprint, New York: Dover, 1970.
Chametzky, Jules. *From the Ghetto: The Fiction of Abraham Cahan.* Amherst: University of Massachusetts Press, 1977.

Anzia Yezierska

1880?–1970

Of the first generation of Jewish American writers who were born in Eastern Europe or on the Lower East Side, Anzia Yezierska was the leading female novelist and short-story writer. She portrayed the Lower East Side ghetto existence from a poor woman's perspective. She exulted in the possibilities of life in America while lamenting the loss of family cohesion, religious observance, and traditional Jewish values that accompanied deracination and pursuit of the dollar. Throughout the body of her work Yezierska reiterated her main theme: the transformation, through great effort, of young immigrant women from greenhorn status to that of educated, productive modern Jewish Americans.

Yezierska was a headstrong woman, reaching out and grabbing with both hands all the experience and opportunity she could manage as she demanded of the world recognition of her individuality and talent. She was a whirlwind, a dynamo. She personified the immigrant's determination to succeed in America. Although she lived for a time among the masses, Yezierska struggled to stand out. She fervently desired to be seen, heard, and read as a unique talent.

Anzia Yezierska was born in a mud hut in the shtetl of Plotzk, in Russian-occupied Poland. She was the daughter of a religious father, Bernard Yezierska, and Pearl, a hard-working, passive mother who was the mainstay of the family. When Anzia was fifteen, the family, dreaming of wealth in America, immigrated to the Lower East Side, where they were only slightly better off than they had been in Europe.

Upon arrival in New York City, the family took or was given the name Mayer; Anzia remained Hattie Mayer until 1910.

The daughters all went to work in sweatshops to help support their studious father and mother. The boys went to school and soon left the ghetto and their family behind. Anzia, the youngest and most sensitive child, was put to work as a live-in maid. Having learned enough English, she quit that demeaning job and found more independent employment sewing in a sweatshop. The workday was long; additionally, she struggled to improve her English by attending night school. At nineteen she was living on her own, an unusual situation for a young Jewish immigrant woman.

Anzia was fractious, sharp-tongued, rebellious, loud, and unpleasant—especially toward men. But she was intelligent and passionate, as well as determined to break out of the life of a wage slave. The great goal of her young life was somehow to achieve autonomy.

Yezierska's night-school teacher, impressed by her intelligence and drive, encouraged her to seek further education. Using her savings, she studied for a year at New York City Normal College, after which she was awarded a four-year scholarship to Teachers College, Columbia University, to learn domestic science in order to teach it to children. Having earned a degree and a teaching certificate in 1904, she found employment on the Lower East Side teaching young girls to cook, clean, and sew. However, she disliked both teaching and her superiors and quickly abandoned the teaching profession. Anzia next decided on a career in the theater and won a scholarship to the prestigious American Academy of Dramatic Arts. Nothing came of this ambition, so she briefly returned to teaching.

Meanwhile, Anzia had married twice. The first, in 1910, was to Jacob Gordon, a German Jewish lawyer, which ended in an annulment within six months. The second (a religious ceremony with no legal backing), in 1911, was to Arnold Levitas, a German Jewish businessman (who later became a teacher), which resulted in her only child, Louise. But that marriage was not a happy one either. Yezierska hated the role of housewife even though she taught domestic science—or maybe because she did. She also had no taste for maternal duties. In 1916 she finally left her husband and agreed that he should take custody of the child. Now she could devote more time to her literary pursuits.

In 1913 Yezierska began to write fiction. (She had previously written only verse.) In 1915 her first story, "Free Vacation House," a powerful attack on the arrogance and condescension of settlement workers, was published in *Forum*. Other short-story publications followed. Yezierska, then in her mid-thirties, turned to creative writing with the passion and determination to succeed that had marked her early life. She quickly learned that life on the Lower East Side was hers to mine. She created a parade of exotic (at least to the general reading public) characters speaking in the fractured Yiddish-inflected English of the ghetto, a language she made sound almost poetic.

Seeking to obtain permission to audit a seminar in social and political thought at Columbia University in 1917, Yezierska met the instructor, the distinguished educator and philosopher John Dewey. A relationship developed between them. She was thirty-seven; he was fifty-eight and married. She became his research assistant, translator of Polish and Yiddish, and lover while they worked together on a project in Philadelphia. Although Dewey wrote many love poems to her, the affair only lasted a year. Much later Yezierska would publish a fictionalized account of the relationship under the title *All I Could Never Be* (1932).

In 1919 Yezierska's short story "The Fat of the Land," originally written for a Columbia University creative writing course and published in a magazine in 1918, was named Best Short Story of 1919 by Edward J. O'Brien, a well-known editor, and was included in his anthology *The Best Short Stories* (1920). (O'Brien even dedicated the volume to Yezierska.) "The Fat of the Land" is the tale of an elderly East Side Jewish mother who is unable to live in the fancy uptown apartment house in which her successful children have "warehoused" her and who must find her way back to the milieu in which she is most comfortable, namely, the Lower East Side.

As a result of the award, in 1920 the firm of Houghton Mifflin decided to publish a collection of Yezierska's ghetto stories under the title *Hungry Hearts*. This book, as well as subsequent works of fiction, received serious critical attention and acclaim. It was clear that the author, as well as the Jewish women in her stories, were not only hungry for food but for love.

Yezierska had arrived on the New York literary scene. She had become a 1920s celebrity. Samuel Goldwyn, himself an immigrant Jew from Russian-occupied Poland, was impressed enough by the boldness and intensity of the stories to purchase the film rights. Anzia went to Hollywood and was both bedazzled and lonely, feeling totally out of place. The movie *Hungry Hearts,* bearing only a general resemblance to the stories, appeared in 1922. She had received a payment of ten thousand dollars and considered herself rich. Later she would receive fifteen thousand dollars for the film rights to her first novel, *Salome of the Tenements.*

Yezierska soon realized that she could not write amid the glitter and sham of Hollywood and wisely returned to her New York City roots. *Salome of the Tenements* came out in 1923. Yezierska found the inspiration for this novel in the romance and subsequent marriage (in 1905) of her friend Rose Pastor, a fiery Jewish socialist orator (nicknamed the "red Yiddish Cinderella") to the millionaire upperclass WASP James Phelps Graham Stokes, who worked on the Lower East Side in a settlement house funded by his family. In Anzia's novel a reporter for the *Ghetto News,* Sonya Vronsky (had Anzia read *Anna Karenina* in Yiddish or English?) is in love with a well-known American philanthropist, John Manning, who works with impoverished immigrants. She sees him as cultured, noble, and heroic and is determined to marry him. His coolness has a touch of John Dewey's character. Manning comes to like Sonya and offers her a job as his secretary. As a result of their daily contact, he falls in love with her and proposes marriage. Sonya soon discovers that her opulent lifestyle is strange and uncomfortable.

Prior to the marriage Sonya had borrowed fifteen hundred dollars from a pawnbroker to buy clothes and fix up her living quarters in order to make herself more attractive to Manning. She promised the loan shark that she would repay the loan and hand over an additional five hundred dollars if she marries her rich suitor. Now the creditor wants his money, and so she pawns her engagement ring. Doing this seems a betrayal, which disturbs her so much that she rejects her husband's love in the sense of feeling unworthy of it. Foolishly, Manning tries to take Sonya by force and is ashamed of himself. In their exchange of harsh words they reveal painful truths about each other.

The marriage seems over and Sonya decides to leave Manning. She tries to get her newspaper job back, but she is turned away. She gets work as a waitress, and then, surprisingly, as a dress designer. Successful in her new employment, she divorces Manning and marries a former acquaintance, Jacques Hollins, who is also a designer. Manning tries to win her back, but she gently rejects him. Sonya has opened a not-for-profit dress shop on the Lower East Side, where she helps immigrant women obtain beautiful clothes to make their lives more pleasurable and to improve their taste. Sonya is at last content.

Sonya is not a likable character. She is conniving and as determined as any gold digger to land Manning. The various plot twists—epilogue to the story of a broken love and a mistaken marriage—detract from what could have been a more convincing tragic tale of a sensitive young woman betraying herself by accepting the material values of a society she barely understands and marrying for money. That part of Sonya's story—the woman who falls—is credible. The rest seems mere verbiage.

More of Yezierska's stories were collected in *Children of Loneliness* (1923). Yezierska's narrative skills generally increased with each novel or collection of stories, that is, at least until her masterpiece, *Bread Givers* (1925), the story of an immigrant girl's maturation and struggle for independence. Sara Smolinsky, surely a stand-in for Anzia, takes on her selfish, mean, domineering father, Reb Smolinsky, who continually bullies his wife and four daughters, denigrates women in general, and insists on total obedience on the part of his wife and children. Smolinsky's excuse for not providing for his family is that he is doing God's work by reading the Torah and studying the Talmud. He is continually preaching to his family. He has reserved an entire room in the small, crowded flat for his studies. Fleeing patriarchal domination, Sara leaves home and lives in poverty while studying. Smolinsky, who arrogantly claims he knows everything about everything, tries his hand as a grocer, but he is duped into buying a worthless store with the family's savings and the enterprise fails miserably. On her own, Sara makes a successful marriage and finds some contentment, but she always feels a sense of guilt for not doing more for her father, who, following his wife's death, has remarried, this time to a domineering, money-grasping woman, which is just what Smolinsky deserves.

In *Bread Givers* (referring to the women in a family) Yezierska wars against the restrictions and ingrained misogyny of Orthodox Judaism. She demands that women be valued for qualities outside the domestic sphere, and that they raise their self-esteem by prizing what they can accomplish outside the kitchen and the nursery. In a sense Sara and other young women in Yezierska's fiction are still sailing for the New World.

In *Bread Givers* Yezierska's descriptions of Lower East Side life are extremely evocative and effective. One can almost taste and smell the place. The portrait of a selfish father, hiding behind his religiosity in order to avoid working, is the most powerful in all of Yezierska's fiction. In Reb Smolinsky she created a character of Dickensian proportions. The story of his fall, embedded as it is in the story of Sara's life—from the age of eleven, when she begins to free herself from his power by becoming a herring seller, to her success in college, teaching, and marriage—is a counter architectonic of the novel. That double helical plot (father and daughter/father vs. daughter) is what makes *Bread Givers,* a seemingly conventional "girl makes good" narrative, so very rich.

Arrogant Beggar (1927) is based on Yezierska's experiences around the time she was studying domestic science at Teachers College. Adele Lindner, a Lower East Side immigrant, loses her job as a salesgirl and is taken into a special home that trains young women for domestic service. The manager of the home, Miss Simon, is cruel to Adele. The girl's benefactor, Mrs. Hellman, a wealthy uptown woman, patronizes her and uses her as a servant in her home, paying her half the wages she would have paid someone else. Adele is attracted to Hellman's handsome son, Arthur. She soon realizes that she has been taken advantage of. She and most of the other young women in the home have hated the idea of becoming servants from the start, and when Adele has a chance to do so she publicly denounces the hypocrisy of the institution.

Adele returns to the Lower East Side, where she is happier in the authentic, warm, and even generous world of the poor. Arthur seeks her out, proposes marriage, and is rejected because Adele knows that the material life they would share would be destructive. Possessions corrupt. Later Adele meets and falls in love with a concert pianist. They will be happy in the nonmaterialistic life they'll share together.

As a satire on " uptown Jews"—the affluent and condescending German American Jews who, at least in Yezierska's fiction, are exploiters of the poor Eastern European immigrant Jews—*Arrogant Beggar* works fairly well. Although the characters are vivid, the locations ring true, and the distrust of organized charities is understandable, the plot is marred by the improbable relationship between Adele and Arthur. Adele is yet another Yezierska heroine who briefly considers marrying above her class and eventually reconsiders.

All I Could Never Be (1932) harks back to Yezierska's affair with John Dewey. The protagonist, Fanya Iwanova, is an individualist with a passion for social justice. Fanya meets a famous professor, Henry Scott, after hearing him lecture about how the immigrants, through their humility, must teach Americans tolerance. Easy for him to say. Scott is in his sixties and he seems to stand for American high culture.

Fanya and Henry become close. He is moved by her intensity and lust for life's experiences, and he falls in love with Fanya. He offers her a job at a research project in Chicago. There he takes the liberty of kissing her, causing the romantic image of Scott to crumble in Fanya's mind. She still cares for him, but the rejected lover gives her the cold shoulder.

It is now ten years later. Fanya, a successful novelist, is utterly disillusioned with life and still feels empty. She tries to involve herself in labor activism as a palliative and even moves out of New York City. Finally she meets a poor immigrant artist and is able to share, to give of herself, thereby finding peace in the process.

Just as Fanya loses the driving passions that have structured her life, Anzia seemed to lose them too with the advent of the Great Depression. Yezierska's talent seemed to fade away. Her rapid fall in popularity, however, was surely due in part to the reading public's declining interest in stories of immigrant hardships early in the century, when there were so many contemporary tales of suffering in the cities and the dust bowl. Also, Yezierska seemed to have overmined the thematic core of her writing. Stories of the struggling immigrant girl overcoming great odds to win respect as a person seemed repetitive.

Publishing was hit hard during the Depression. Yezierska's royalties dried up. The stock market crash blew away her investments. She did get some work with the WPA Writers' Project. A small legacy from a friend enabled her to continue writing fiction. She moved to a town in New Hampshire, but she found that she couldn't write there; she needed the stimulus of New York City.

Yezierska's last long work was her fictionalized autobiography *Red Ribbon on a White Horse* (1950), which, despite an introduction by W. H. Auden, received little critical attention. The main impression this work leaves the reader is that Yezierska was never content with her life, her lot, and her Golden Land. Anzia Yezierska faded to obscurity even as she kept writing. She published her last story, "Take Up Your Bed and Walk," in the *Chicago Jewish Forum* (1969). After her death the women's movement rediscovered her, her early work finding resonance again in the feminist struggle for equality. Like Yezierska's heroines, a generation of women were going to "be somebody."

Yezierska's great achievement was her ability to depict the difficult life led by Jewish immigrant women who came to America hoping for love, respect, individual identity, and some economic independence, only to have those hopes turn into dreams deferred. She did this while brilliantly recreating in words the noises, smells, and grinding poverty of the Lower East Side, as well as the hopes and aspirations of young Jewish women immigrants at the beginning of the twentieth century.

Additional Reading

Henriksen, Louise Levitas. *Anzia Yezierska: A Writer's Life.* New Brunswick, N.J.: Rutgers University Press, 1988.

Schoen, Carol B. *Anzia Yezierska.* Boston: Twayne, 1982.

Yezierska, Anzia. *All I Could Never Be.* New York: Brewer, Warren and Putnam, 1932.

———. *Arrogant Beggar.* Reprint, Durham, N.C.: Duke University Press, 1996.

———. *Bread Givers.* Reprint, New York: Persea, 1975.

———. *Children of Loneliness: Stories of Immigrant Life in America.* New York: Funk and Wagnalls, 1923.

———. *"How I Found America": The Collected Stories of Anzia Yezierska.* New York: Persea, 1991.

———. *Hungry Hearts and Other Stories.* Reprint, New York: Penguin, 1997.

———. *Red Ribbon on a White Horse* (autobiography). Reprint, New York: Persea, 1987.

———. *Salome of the Tenements.* Reprint, Urbana: University of Illinois Press, 1995.

Rose Cohen

1880–1925?

Like her friend Anzia Yezierska, Rose Cohen was a writer who experienced a love-hate relationship with her cultural and religious background, on the one hand, and her desire to find accommodation for her work and herself in the broader context of American life, on the other. Also like Yezierska, Cohen found recognition and success writing in English, her adopted language. Both women worked very hard to master English and develop their craft. Both only achieved recognition well into their thirties. It all ended tragically for Cohen when, it appears, after at least one previous attempt at suicide, she took her own life. Her literary masterpiece, *Out of the Shadow* (1918), is a brilliant, vivid, slightly fictionalized account of her early life in Europe and living on the Lower East Side.

Rose Gollup Cohen landed in New York's Lower East Side in 1912, having traveled from a Russian shtetl in what is now Belarus and eventually settled in a tenement on Cherry Street with her parents, two sisters, two brothers, and an aunt. The family was jampacked into a two-bedroom flat. Her father was a tailor. Rose received a meager primary education and learned English in the public schools, but she was soon put to work as a seamstress. According to the 1900 census, Rose Gollup was still living at home, where she was called "Rosie." As was typical for the immigrant family, everyone went to work as soon as they could. The family focus on the boys was also typical, both of whom eventually received college educations.

As a teenage worker, Rose briefly became involved in union activities connected with the United Hebrew Trades. When there was no work in the garment industry, she slaved as a domestic. Rose was not a very healthy person, and part of her illness may have been psychological. At the Henry Street Settlement the seventeen-year-old met and became a protégée of Lillian Wald, who referred the unwell to the Presbyterian Hospital uptown. For the first time Rose became aware of the world outside the ghetto.

Through Wald Rose was also able to join a workers' co-op, which made shirtwaists. In 1902 she began work as an assistant teacher of machine sewing at the Manhattan Trade School for Girls. She continued to further her education, taking courses at the Educational Alliance and elsewhere. She married Joseph Cohen, quit work, and gave birth to a daughter, Evelyn. At the age of twenty-two, feeling confident about her English skills, she slowly began to write. A few pieces were published. Encouraged, she produced her masterpiece *Out of the Shadow.* Reviews were excellent. Cohen was recognized as a writer with genuine talent and as a spokesperson for the immigrant woman's experience. Cohen's success with her autobiographical novel probably influenced Anzia Yezierska. Cohen's stories also found acceptance; one entitled "Natalka's Portion" was included in *The Best Short Stories of 1922.* In the summer of 1923 and 1924 Cohen was a resident writer at the MacDowell Colony in Petersborough, New Hampshire. Then she suddenly disappeared from sight.

Out of the Shadow is Cohen's personal history. It begins with her character Rahel's earliest memories in Russia, her danger-filled escape with Aunt Masha to Europe, the illness-ridden voyage to America on an English ship, and arrival at Castle Garden Immigration Center, where her father met them.

Rahel finds that her father is no longer the pious Jew he was in their native village. They live as roomers in an apartment rented by a woman who brings home piecework and takes care of her baby. Rahel quickly learns that all one does in America is work, eat, and sleep. Shortly after her arrival, Rahel's father puts her to work as a baster in the one-room sweatshop in which he is employed. She works fourteen hours a day, six days a week. Her beleaguered father, who is trying to save enough money to bring over the rest of the family, beats her when angered. He himself is beaten up by a gang of anti-Semitic gentile boys. Others throw stones at passing Jews or overturn the pushcarts of Jewish peddlers. To protect himself from anti-Semites, Rahel's father shaves his beard to disguise his Jewishness. Rahel is saddened by what she perceives as his loss of faith.

As Rahel begins to mature, her boss makes a sexual pass at her, and when she refuses his advances, he fires her. Her next employer cheats her out of money, forcing her to find yet another sweatshop to work in. Over a year later Rahel's mother and siblings arrive and the family moves to larger quarters on Broome Street. This is strictly a business move; although they are already crowded, they are now able to take in boarders.

Rahel learns English more quickly and correctly than any other member of the family. She is becoming "Americanized." She even convinces her Orthodox Jewish mother to give up her required wig and let her hair grow out. When the clothing-manufacturing trade slows down, the family has to be fed, so Rahel, now fourteen years old, becomes a live-in maid for a family on Clinton Street. She is given little food and a meager salary of twelve dollars per week in exchange for working from dawn to late at night six days a week. In a few months Rahel realizes that she would rather work in the sweatshop than be exploited and earn slave wages in this household.

Undernourished and anemic, Rahel falls ill and is unable to work. At home she begins to read books in Yiddish and finds that she loves Dickens in translation. Now sixteen years old, she meets a young grocer who wants to marry her. The family is ecstatic, but when Rahel gradually realizes that marriage includes sex, she backs off, feeling that she could not do that with a man she did not love. The family is distraught.

Rahel now begins to write in Yiddish and teaches herself to read English. She meets Lillian Wald, who enrolls her in a class at the Henry Street Settlement, but Rahel is ill again and must go to a hospital. After three months in the Presbyterian Hospital, where she is obliged to eat nonkosher food and tries to read the Bible in English, she returns home determined to go to night school at the Educational Alliance on East Broadway. Ill again, she is sent to convalesce in the country, where her gentile friends call her Ruth.

At seventeen Rahel is back at work in a sweatshop, but Wald intervenes and finds her a place in a school where she learns dressmaking.

This leads to a dressmaker's position in a large Fifth Avenue store, but soon she is back in the factories. At eighteen she begins a friendship with a young Jewish man who has converted to Christianity. Her father is rabid and tries to act as matchmaker again but fails. Rahel goes back to work, but her story ends with the twenty-year-old Rahel—and the reader—hoping that she will find happiness someday.

Out of the Shadow does not achieve a satisfactory closure. The ending is abrupt. The focus unexpectedly shifts to a bright brother. Rahel's future remains vague. But the narrative is always engaging, and although somewhat self-pitying, it successfully portrays the feelings and experiences of a very young, sensitive female Jewish immigrant in New York City at the beginning of the twentieth century.

Additional Reading

Cohen, Rose. *Out of the Shadow: A Russian Jewish Girlhood on the Lower East Side.* Reprint, Ithaca, N.Y.: Cornell University Press, 1995.

Marcus Eli Ravage

1884–1965

Born in the town of Valsuli in Rumania, Marcus Eli Ravage came to the Lower East Side in 1900. As a youth of sixteen he peddled chocolates on the street, tended bar, and worked as a shirt-sewing operator in a sweatshop. Like thousands of other immigrants, he learned English in night school and gained additional knowledge by attending public lectures and by seeking out and mixing with Lower East Side intellectuals in teahouses and coffee shops.

A voracious reader, Ravage eventually became a journalist and political commentator. Among the books he published are: *Five Men of Frankfurt: The Story of the Rothschilds* (1929), a history of the great Jewish banking family; *The Malady of Europe* (1923), a study of the intricacies and failures of post–World War I European politics; *The Story of Teapot Dome* (1924), which dealt with the great Harding administration political scandal; and *Empress Innocence* (1931), a biography of Napoleon's second empress, Marie Louise. Ravage's most important book was his personal story *An American in the Making: The Life Story of an Immigrant* (1917), in which he described his youth on the Lower East Side. This book was for many years used as a text in American high schools.

Possessing fluency in several languages, Ravage served as an outstanding European correspondent for *The Nation*. He also wrote for the *New Republic* and *Harper's* magazine. Several European periodicals used his services as well.

An American in the Making depicts the disappointment many immigrants experienced once in America. It shows the deterioration of religious strictures, such as Sabbath worship and kashruth, as well as Eastern European culture, taste, respect for elders, family ties, and various other ethical and moral qualities that had been inculcated in European Jewry for hundreds of years. The immigrants Ravage portrayed seemed adrift and demoralized.

After the adventure of getting to America and experiencing Ellis Island, Ravage quickly came to the realization that he hated America. His father, learning that his son was hungry and was renting part of a bed in a cousin's apartment that slept twenty-five men and women, offered to bring him home. Ravage considered accepting the offer but chose not to be defeated. There was opportunity in America, and democracy and classlessness held sway among the workers and even the shop owners. Also, the food was astonishingly varied and delicious in all seasons, provided one could afford what seemed exorbitant prices. In retrospect, Ravage decided that on the whole America wasn't such a bad place after all. Clearly, a part of Ravage's problem with New York was that the young man was homesick, something immigrants from many lands also experience today.

Some people took advantage of Ravage's youth and greenhorn status, while others out and out cheated him, but he made good friends and he continually learned. Discovering the Yiddish theater, he found diversion, beauty, and wisdom in the plays, the actors, and fellow members of the audience with whom he debated the merits of a production.

After both of Ravage's parents had died in Rumania within a two-week period, his brothers joined him in New York City. School beckoned. Ravage studied English, German, and algebra in high school until he was able to pass the Regents exams. The Rumanian immigrant community began to look up to him as a person with a future. Ravage was accepted by the University of Missouri at Columbia. Journeying west by train, he came to appreciate the size and diversity of his newly adopted country. At the university he had trouble making acquaintances, playing sports, and enjoying food that seemed tasteless to him, but he endured, made friends, and graduated in three years. He now felt he was an American. His future looked promising and it would definitely not be on the Lower East Side.

An American in the Making is an immigrant success story, but, as Ravage admits, Americanization came at a price. Ghetto relatives and friends no longer viewed him as one of them. As *An American in the Making* ends, European ways on the Lower East Side now seem strange to the young Jewish man from out west.

Additional Reading

Ravage, Marcus Eli. *An American in the Making: The Life Story of an Immigrant.* Reprint, New York: Dover, 1971.

Samuel Ornitz

1890–1957

Samuel Ornitz was a compassionate writer who was deeply committed to social causes. He had the courage of his convictions and used his skills for the betterment of humankind. Ornitz made his living as a screenwriter. In the early 1950s—as one of the notorious Hollywood Ten, a group of writers accused of being communists during the McCarthy-era witch hunt—he refused to give up his constitutional right not to incriminate himself and others by stating that he was now or had been a member of the Communist Party, or that he knew of colleagues who were members. Ornitz affirmed that even posing such questions was wrong. For his courage he went to prison. Unlike other blacklisted Hollywood writers, he chose not to write under a pseudonym after being released from prison. Samuel Ornitz was a true champion of civil liberties.

Samuel Badisch Ornitz was born on Hester Street, the same street on which the great modern sculptor Sir Jacob Epstein had been born ten years earlier. Ornitz's parents were newly arrived Polish Jewish immigrants. He attended the Henry Street Public School and a Jewish school for religious instruction. He also took cultural courses at the Henry Street Settlement. After two years of study at City College, New York, he selected social work as his initial career choice, hoping to help prisoners, children, and the poor. At twenty-four he married Sadie Lesser, with whom he had two sons.

Abandoning social work, Ornitz began to write, eventually winding up in Hollywood, where he collaborated with some of the finest screenwriters of his time, including Nathanael West and Bud

Schulberg. Ornitz wrote screenplays for Paramount, RKO, Universal, and Republic. He was also instrumental in founding the Screenwriters Guild.

Although he wrote more than thirty screenplays, Ornitz was a writer of fiction before he became a screenwriter. In 1923 he anonymously published his best-known novel, *Haunch, Paunch and Jowl*. Set on the Lower East Side, it chronicles the way immigrants fought their way out of poverty. The funny, picaresque novel is anticapitalist. It centers on New York City crime and political corruption, particularly the misdeeds of an obese judge referred to in political cartoons as "Haunch, Paunch and Jowl."

In a first-person narrative the protagonist, Meyer Hirsch, a streetwise boy, relates his rise from impoverished tenement life to a powerful New York judgeship. Meyer is a child of Russian Jewish immigrants. He is a brawler and, from the age of nine, a gang leader on Ludlow Street. His father fled Russia to escape military service and now works as a sewing-machine operator, while Meyer's mother struggles to keep the family together. At fourteen Meyer is a thief, mainly stealing food because he is always hungry. His gang goes in for extortion of shopkeepers. Meyer, as the general, organizes the Jewish gangs to wage war against the Irish gangs. Ornitz's description of gang warfare among Jewish and Irish teenagers is vivid. While still in his teens, Meyer frequents the prostitutes on Allen Street. The gang, the former Ludlow Street Streetcarers (named for hitching dangerous rides) are now called the Ludlow Street Don Juans.

Finishing public schooling, Meyer is sent to City College on Twenty-third Street because Uncle Philip has decreed that he is to be a lawyer. He is put to work as a "runner," seeking clients for a shyster lawyer. Meyer lusts after women and worries about contracting a venereal disease. At eighteen his admiring pals are out stealing law books for Meyer to study. He becomes a Democratic Party gopher and buyer of votes. He has learned that his intelligence could take him far in a city run by corrupt, small-brained men.

Now a licensed lawyer, Meyer rises high in ghetto politics. His love life is polarized: he worships the "pure" Esther but sleeps with the sexy maid Gretel. To Meyer's great disappointment Esther marries his enemy, the Irishman Finn. But Meyer Hirsch is now so powerful he "makes" aldermen, state assemblymen, and congressmen, all of whom remain in his debt. Grown fat from his opulent life, Hirsch is nicknamed "Haunch, Paunch and Jowl." By means of extortion Hirsch wins the judgeship of the Superior Criminal Court and the world kowtows to him. However, he is blackmailed by Gretel into marrying her, thus ending his career (because he married his servant). Hirsch lives on in bitterness, luxury, and gourmandizing, consoled only by his mistress, a former prostitute.

In *Haunch, Paunch, and Jowl* Ornitz deliciously and savagely anatomizes and satirizes the darker underbelly of the Jewish ghetto world: corrupt Lower East Side politics; the predatory legal profession scavenging for clients on the streets; religious hypocrisy; the vicious labor-versus-manufacturer wars, union busting and union corruption; mendaciousness; rampant graft; and a judiciary that is for sale.

The style of the book is particularly interesting in that it may contain the first use of a Joycean stream-of-consciousness narrative in American literature. *Haunch, Paunch and Jowl* was Ornitz's most popular literary effort. Its boldness, sexiness, Rabelaisian qualities, and engrossing descriptions of the Lower East Side make it a minor masterpiece. It could very well have influenced Michael Gold in his later novel *Jews without Money* (1930).

Ornitz's second novel appeared in 1927, just before he left for Hollywood. *A Yankee Passional* is a long, somewhat allegorical tale about a New England mystic named Daniel Matthews, a devout and committed Roman Catholic convert from Protestantism who establishes a religious movement that develops a large following. He also founds a New York City home for boys. The Vatican is dismayed by what he is doing and fundamentalist Protestants hate him because he opposes the entrance of the United States into World War I. Eventually the American Guardians, an organization modeled after the Ku Klux Klan, assassinate him. Thus, a passionately good person, doing the work of God, is martyred by organized evil. *A Yankee Passional* is overplotted, often didactic, and too digressive, but it is a powerful attack on the destructive power of organized religion and the way it quashes and destroys true spirituality. The novel also attacks the bigoted quasi-political, quasi-underground but always self-appointed guardians of American morality. In another time and place the saintly martyr Matthews could have founded a new religion, one more compassionate than current ones.

Ornitz's last novel, *Bride of the Sabbath* (1951), is a long historical narrative that brings to vivid life the background, ethical inheritance, and political consciousness that led the children of Jewish immigrants to become passionate, deeply committed American liberals of the mid-twentieth century.

Bride of the Sabbath is also a bildungsroman following the growth and development of a young Jewish man. The subject of the novel is the maturation and education of Saul Cramer, a sensitive boy from New York's Lower East Side who, raised in an Orthodox Jewish family, is molded into a liberal American as a result of the Darwinian cauldron of illness, pain, suffering, hunger, drunkenness, cruelty, corruption, violent anti-Semitism, self-hatred, and death that shaped his early environment. In this novel Ornitz reexamined the time and place of his youth, writing about the rich and variegated ghetto culture that first sheltered him and then inculcated a sense of moral conscience, compassion, and social consciousness that informed his life and work, priming him for his artistic success in the wider world.

Bride of the Sabbath begins with a finely detailed panorama of Lower East Side Jewish life in 1898 viewed from a child's perspective. Saul Cramer grows up alternately loving and hating his Jewishness. He is a brilliant child. At the age of thirteen he gets a job as a bookkeeper for a sweatshop, all the while continuing his studies in school. He has to buy a forged set of working papers to do so. On the document his first name is given as Saal, and that name becomes the appellation of his alter ego.

Night classes permit him to enter college. His childhood sweetheart, Pauline, and he both drift away from Jewishness. Saul begins to read English novels, attends plays by George Bernard Shaw, and affects an English accent. Although Pauline is determined that he will be a doctor, he decides on a career as a social worker. Angered, the materialistic Pauline throws him over for a wealthy dress-shop owner. Heartbroken, Saul finds temporary solace with a socialist girlfriend, Becky, but she spends too much time on the speaker's platform and they eventually break up.

Now Saul is completely transformed into Saal. He has affairs with gentile women, pursues his career as a public advocate in the merciless and bigoted court system, and tries to write about his experiences. Jewishness seems to him an unbearable burden. To the dancer Nancy Fitzgerald the protean Saal becomes "Sean." When Becky resurfaces, his emotional life is suspended between Nancy the Catholic artist and Becky the ardent Jewish socialist. He chooses Nancy for his wife. She tries to make him convert to Christianity and he tries to win her over to his brand of liberalism. She becomes a lay nun and Saal attempts to embrace her religion out of his continuing love for her. In the end Saul finds peace in a chaste, Tolstoyan version of Christianity.

The shortcomings of *Bride of the Sabbath* weigh the novel down. It lacks a degree of satiric humor that some of the situations cry out for. Most of all, it is far too splenetic, such that the reader senses exaggeration where Ornitz intends verisimilitude. Ornitz knows the tragedies of Jewish history only too well, but in recounting them he slows up the continuity of the plot once too often. However, as a sociological portrait of a generation, an illustration of the pain of assimilation, a truthful depiction of the land mines in Jewish-Gentile relations, and as a bildungsroman anchored in a unique time and place, *Bride of the Sabbath* deserves to be remembered and read.

Ornitz was working on a novel when he died. It was neither finished nor published as a fragment. He was perhaps a paradigm for how socially conscious liberalism became the secular Jewish religion for much of the twentieth century and up to the present. Ornitz did not live to see the later cold war revelations of Stalinist oppression, terror, mass murder, and anti-Semitism—from which, one suspects, he would have recoiled. And Samuel Ornitz never renounced his earlier commitment to the Communist Party.

Additional Reading

Ornitz, Samuel. *Bride of the Sabbath.* New York: Rinehart, 1951.
——. *Haunch, Paunch and Jowl.* Reprint, New York: Markus Weiner, 1986.

Marie Ganz

1891–1968

Marie Ganz was a fiery Lower East Side labor organizer and anarchist who wrote one of the most exciting and insightful fictionalized autobiographies of her time. *Rebels: Into Anarchy—And Out Again* (1919) is the story of the maturation of a young immigrant woman on New York City's Lower East Side.

Marie Ganz was born in a shtetl located in a part of the province of Galicia in Austrian Poland that is now in Ukraine. Her father, Lazarus Ganz, came to New York City in 1894. After two years of hard work and scrimping, he brought his wife, his daughter, Marie—who was then five years old—and a younger son, Schmeel, to America, exchanging a comfortable and healthy life in an agricultural area for the crowded, filthy, disease-ridden world of the Lower East Side—and a life of abject poverty. Three years later Lazarus Ganz, a pushcart peddler who hawked bananas, died.

From the age of eight Marie worked after school and on weekends alongside her mother doing piecework so the small family could survive. As was customary for immigrant children, when she was thirteen Marie left school to work full time. She found employment as a delivery person for a dressmaker who catered to the uptown carriage trade. As a result, she came to realize how enormously unequal life in America was. Her next job was in a sweatshop, where, after work, she hung out with radical students and read political literature. She became an anarchist and a labor-union organizer at the sweatshop where she worked, which naturally led to her being fired.

Ganz found a niche for herself in the union movement. She championed the rights of female workers and the needs of unemployed women. The all-male leadership of the unions was always less concerned for the female workers in their industries than for their male counterparts. Ganz helped raise the gender consciousness of the Lower East Side union leadership.

Ganz was an effective orator, especially adept at whipping up Jewish crowds on Rutgers Place, in the shadow of the Forward Building. Ganz took as her brief the achievement of fair wages and equal opportunity for the entire immigrant Jewish population of the Lower East Side, especially the large numbers of Italian female workers.

Ganz's most shocking action was not as a labor organizer but rather as an anarchist. In 1914, a loaded pistol in her hand, she marched at the head of a crowd to the Standard Oil Building in Manhattan. There she announced that she was going to shoot John D. Rockefeller "like a dog" because his mining company in Colorado used thugs to beat down the striking miners. Fortunately for Rockefeller and Ganz, the titan of industry was not in. Ganz then left word with a secretary that she would be back to get him another time. The agitprop theatrical made for good press. The police did not take Ganz too seriously. She was arrested on charges of disorderly conduct and sentenced to sixty days in jail, which was reduced to thirty.

After the Rockefeller fiasco, Ganz remained relatively peaceful. She began to seek legal methods to achieve social gains. In 1917 she supported American intervention in the war on the side of the Allies, although many of her friends were disturbed that the United States was allying itself with despotic imperial Russia, the most oppressive regime in Europe. In 1919 Ganz married the journalist Nat Ferber and also published *Rebels*. Her radical fires dampened if not entirely extinguished, she slipped out of sight.

Rebels is a lively, upbeat saga of a young immigrant woman's first quarter century of life. Unlike most immigrant memoirs, it does not dwell on the painful or the pitiful, although there is much sadness in Ganz's early life. The main item on Ganz's agenda is political: identifying and combating inequality. She paints vivid sketches of landlords, penniless boarders, funeral mourners, the homeless and the hungry, sweatshop tyrants and beleaguered workers, industrial workers plying their craft and skills, and the exhausting lives of women of the ghetto. Ganz has the ability to isolate and display the special characteristics of her subjects in order to distinguish them from the mass of humanity that flows past her. The ghetto wedding of Zalmon Eckstoff, for example, is a symphony of mishaps, gluttony, and greed. Ganz's word-picture has all the detail of a Brueghel painting—and it's funny to boot!

The first tragedy marking Marie's childhood is the death of her father, who is exhausted from overwork and lack of proper nourishment. The second is the death of her little brother, who had agreed to help the fatherless family by working as a pushcart peddler.

Marie grows older and wiser. She meets a group of Russian Jewish socialists. These intellectuals widen Ganz's world. During a rent strike she discovers that she has the ability to rouse the ghetto dwellers to take action. In 1914, while participating in a riot where protesters are clubbed by police, Ganz is ready to kill the cops, whom she sees as the tools of the capitalists. Ganz has no admiration for Emma Goldman, the leading anarchist of her time, whom she accuses of being insincere and having selfishly sold out in order to live a life of luxury. Ganz's contemporary perspective on Goldman is clearly at odds with the way history has portrayed the famous radical.

Ganz's mother tries to marry off her daughter to a boorish clod. Marie refuses despite her mother's tears. Ganz's description of the disgusting suitor is worthy of the pen of Dickens.

When Ganz was arrested, tried, and convicted as a result of her attempt on the life of John D. Rockefeller, she was sent to the women's prison on Blackwell's Island, located in the East River. It is a grim place, and Ganz's description of the degraded lives of women prisoners in New York City in the period before America's entry into World War I is a piece of classic reportage. She clearly was an autodidact, possessing the intelligence and ability to teach herself to write like the best muckraking novelists of her generation.

In 1917–18, when the United States began drafting young immigrants for Army combat in the battlefields of France, Ganz became less critical of her government. Proud of the young men she had known who emerged from the Jewish ghetto to fight for their adopted country, she came to see the United States in a new and better light. It is our loss that her interest in writing ended with her declining involvement in radical politics. It is a pity that, following the success of *Rebels,* she never started a new career as a writer of fiction like Anzia Yezierska.

Additional Reading

Ganz, Marie. *Rebels: Into Anarchy—And Out Again.* Reprint, Millwood, N.Y.: Kraus 1976.

Marsh, Margaret S. *Anarchist Women, 1870–1920.* Philadelphia: Temple University Press, 1981.

Ben Hecht

1893–1964

Ben Hecht was the enfant terrible of American letters in the first half of the twentieth century. He was political clear across the spectrum, making enemies on the Right as well as on the Left. He angered American Jews, moderate Israeli Zionists, and the British government with his strident support of Jewish extremist attacks on British troops and United Nations personnel in Palestine. If Hecht was consistently opposed to anything, it was to censorship of literature, art, and film by either the government or self-appointed guardians of public morality.

The best word to describe Hecht is iconoclast. He delighted in shocking, scandalizing, and outraging friend and foe alike. For the first forty years of his life he hardly thought of himself as a Jew, but the rise of Hitler in Germany during the 1930s changed Hecht's mind. In the wake of murderous anti-Semitism, Hecht not only acknowledged his Jewishness but strove to serve the Jewish people in their greatest hour of need since the destruction of the Temple by the Romans in A.D. 70. He battled for the establishment of the State of Israel using his own brand of ammunition: brilliant writing and persuasive talk. His love for the new state turned to bitterness when he came to believe that Zionist leaders did not do enough to rescue Hungarian Jews from the Holocaust late in World War II.

Even though he never attended college, Hecht became a successful novelist, playwright, journalist, and screenwriter. His star has sunk below the horizon now, but in his own lifetime Hecht became one of the most famous American literary and entertainment figures—quite an achievement by someone from the Lower East Side.

Benjamin Hecht's father, Joseph Hecht, was a garment worker whose specialty was cutting cloth to patterns. He and his future wife, Sarah Swernofski, had immigrated to the Lower East Side from Minsk, Belarus, then part of the Russian Empire. The family language was Yiddish. The Hechts married on the Lower East Side in 1892 and Ben was born the next year. Ben only attended the Broome Street Elementary School from 1898 to 1899, before Joseph Hecht, seeking better employment, moved the family (which now included another son) to Chicago. Four years later Joseph Hecht uprooted the family again and moved to Racine, Wisconsin, where Ben attended high school. In Racine Joseph became a successful manufacturer, producing women's clothing based on his own designs. On the road much of the time, Joseph did not have much effect on Hecht's childhood. Sarah was busy managing the store outlet in downtown Racine. As a result, the boys, Ben and Peter, were pretty much on their own. One summer they even managed a brief show-business career as trapeze artists with a traveling circus. At other times Ben Hecht worked in the family store.

After graduating from high school in 1910, Hecht moved to Chicago, lived with relatives, and started a career in journalism. He was an excellent reporter who worked on several Chicago papers. After World War I Hecht was sent to cover Berlin for the *Chicago Daily News*. There he wrote his first and most successful novel, *Erik Dorn* (1921). It was a sensational debut for Hecht as a serious writer. None of the other eight novels he wrote in his lifetime proved as successful. One, *A Jew in Love* (1931), a cruel satire on Hecht's "friends" in show business and publishing, evidences a degree of Jewish self-hatred in Hecht.

The eponymous hero of *Erik Dorn* is an American version of Dostoevski's underground man, jaded and made distraught by darkening times resulting from postwar chaos and revolution. Dorn joins in the fighting, finds and loses love, kills, and plans to return home to Chicago, as cynical about life as when he left. Dorn first stops off to reclaim the wife he had left behind when he went to Germany. She informs him that she no longer loves him, has divorced him in his absence, and will marry another. At the place of his birth in lower Manhattan, Dorn shares a house with his old father, Isaac, with whom, it appears, he will live out a lonely life.

Hecht moved back to New York City in 1924, living for a while on Henry Street across from the Henry Street Settlement. Here Hecht began a brilliant career as a playwright, collaborating with his fellow journalist and friend Charles MacArthur, the subject of a later biography by Hecht (*Charlie: The Improbable Life and Times of Charles MacArthur* [1957]). Together they wrote one of the most famous American plays of the 1920s, *The Front Page* (1928), a witty drama set in the pressroom of a Chicago courthouse and full of Runyonesque characters. Five film versions under various titles have helped to perpetuate the popularity of the play.

Hecht and MacArthur's second most famous play, *Twentieth Century* (1932), is a screwball comedy about theater people that also became a successful film. *Jumbo* (1935), a circus extravaganza written for the impresario Billy Rose, had a nine-month run on Broadway and later was turned into a film (1962), although Hecht never cared for the play. Other plays, often written with collaborators, were less successful.

Hollywood money wooed Hecht west. Alone or with MacArthur, Hecht wrote some seventy screenplays. The best-known films are: *Scarface* (1932), *Design for Living* (1933), *Twentieth Century* (1934), *Gunga Din* (1939), *Wuthering Heights* (1939), *The Outlaw* (1941), *Spellbound* (1945), *Notorious* (1946), and *A Farewell to Arms* (1957). Hecht was the uncredited rewrite person on many other well-known films.

Ben Hecht published an autobiography, reminiscences, and letters: *A Child of the Century* (1954), *Gaily, Gaily* (1963), and *Letters from Bohemia* (1964). His last play, *Winkleburg* (1958), is also autobiographical.

A Child of the Century is a vast, entertaining collection of revised essays, anecdotes, revenge pieces, and character sketches of incidents, remembrances, friends, relations, and acquaintances spanning his childhood days on the Lower East Side, Chicago, and Racine to the beginning of the 1950s. The text reads more like an impressionistic novel than a conventional autobiography; some of it is clearly fictionalized for literary effect. A large portion of the book contains an account of Hecht's mission as a fund-raiser and arms dealer for the "terrorist" Jewish organization Irgun Zvai Leumi, which fought the British, the Arabs, and sometimes even other Israelis. *A Child of the Century* contains misinformation and exaggeration, but the writing, as always in Hecht's work, is provocative and engaging.

In 1915 Hecht married Marie Armstrong, a fellow Chicago reporter, reviewer, and poet. Marie was an Episcopalian. The marriage resulted in one daughter. They were divorced eleven years later, and Hecht married Rose Caylor, a Russian-born, Yiddish-speaking Jewish writer, with whom he had one daughter.

Hecht, who once improbably claimed that he had never experienced anti-Semitism in his life, and who claimed to have had little to do with Judaism, nevertheless was drawn back to the Lower East Side late in life and lived for a while on Henry Street, where he could absorb the energy and social consciousness of the ghetto.

Thanks to his fund-raising, speeches, and jawboning, Ben Hecht did more to help Jewish refugees from the Holocaust and to ensure the survival of the nascent State of Israel than any other American Jew in the twentieth century. As much as anything, it was the abiding love of his Jewish parents and Rose Hecht that motivated the writer to become arguably the most effective propagandist the Jewish state ever had. In 1966, at Hecht's funeral service at Temple Rodeph Sholom in New York City, among the eulogists was Menachem Begin, the then prime minister of Israel.

Additional Reading

Hecht, Ben. *A Child of the Century.* New York: Simon and Schuster, 1954.
———. *Gaily, Gaily.* New York: Doubleday, 1963.
MacAdams, William. *Ben Hecht: The Man Behind the Legend.* New York: Scribners, 1990.
Martin, Jeffrey Brown. *Ben Hecht: Hollywood Screenwriter.* Ann Arbor, Mich.: UMI Research Press, 1985.

Michael Gold

1893–1967

Michael Gold, the author of *Jews without Money,* the most famous proletarian narrative to emerge from the Great Depression, was born Itzok Isaac Granich on the Lower East Side. In school his name was changed to Irving and then Irwin—each change less Jewish-sounding. In 1921 he adopted the pen name of Michael Gold; he did so either because he admired an older radical with that name, a Civil War veteran and the father of a friend, or (more likely) because he tried to avoid being swept up in the U.S. government raids on radical organizations and individuals following the Red Scare that developed in America following the end of World War I. The Russian Revolution of 1917 and the subsequent rise of international communism polarized the American public in the 1920s and 1930s even more than the early stages of the cold war had polarized it from the late 1940s through the 1960s.

Gold's parents, Chaim Granich and Gittel Schwartz Granich, immigrated to the Lower East Side from Rumania. Gold's father learned how to make men's suspenders; as a small manufacturer, he contracted to make one small part of the set. Eventually his storefront business failed and he had to work the streets as a pushcart peddler in order to support his family. Gold never forgot his father's humiliation and was never able to believe in the capitalist system again.

As was the custom for poor children at the time, Gold left school early. At the age of twelve he had a full-time job with the Adams Express Company as a night porter and teamster, which at that time involved driving a horse or a team of horses hitched to a delivery wagon. He also worked as an errand boy in the garment industry, a shipping clerk, and a printer's devil. In 1912 he began to study journalism at night at New York University. In 1914 he took some classes at Harvard. That year, at a rally of unemployed men and women held at Union Square in Lower Manhattan, Gold, who was simply a bystander at first, was roughed up in a brutal charge by police armed with truncheons. From that moment until the end of his life Gold remained a radical.

In 1917 Gold began to write for the distinguished weekly journal *The Masses* under the mentorship of radical intellectual Max Eastman. Gold joined the Communist Party after moving to Greenwich Village, where he produced a stream of political poems, articles, and stories. The United States entered World War I in 1917 and instituted a military draft. Early in 1918 Gold fled to Mexico to avoid being conscripted. There he worked on a ranch and in oil fields. He returned to New York after the war. Gold edited *The Liberator* in 1921, following which he moved to San Francisco.

Writing plays was Gold's main literary pursuit in the early 1920s. His avant-garde friends included Theodore Dreiser, Eugene O'Neill, and Susan Glaspell. Eugene O'Neill's Provincetown Players in Greenwich Village put on some of Gold's plays, with only modest success. John Reed, the most famous American Communist Party member and the only American to be buried in the Kremlin, was another friend. Unlike many of his acquaintances, Gold was never a communist theorist. He didn't work at understanding Marx. He simply embraced and endorsed popular Marxist views, which he presented in the most inflammatory way he could. Gold's lifelong commitment to radicalism came from the heart, not the mind.

In 1925 Gold traveled to the Soviet Union to study theater and write more radical plays. Returning to the Unites States, undaunted by conditions in the Soviet Union, Gold founded the radical New Playwrights Group, which produced early plays by John Dos Passos and other Leftist writers.

When, at the urging of H. L. Mencken, *Jews without Money* was published in 1930—a year in which the Depression gripped the nation—Gold had been working on the book for a dozen or so years. It was an immediate success, going through eleven editions in the first year alone. After struggling as a writer for so long, Gold was now hailed as "the American Gorki." The book has not been out of print since its original publication, having touched the collective American heart. The short-lived proletarian literature movement—which produced literature written for and by workers—had found its masterpiece.

Lauded by such distinguished American writers and critics as Edmund Wilson and Sinclair Lewis, upon the resignation of Max Eastman in 1925 Gold became coeditor of the *New Masses*. Soon the old Lower East Side street fighter began long feuds with other American writers when he calumniated (in print) the likes of Ernest Hemingway, Archibald MacLeish, Robinson Jeffers, Sherwood Anderson, Granville Hicks, and Thornton Wilder. For Gold conventionally liberal writers were sellouts and tools of the rich capitalists.

In 1933 Gold began to write for the long-lived and once popular American Communist newspaper the *Daily Worker*. In *The Hollow Men* (1941) Gold attacked writers who had abandoned communism following the cynical insincere German-Russian nonaggression pact of 1939. Despite revelations of Stalinist terror and anti-Semitism, Gold, like Samuel Ornitz, remained loyal to communism all his life. Following America's entry into World War II, Gold's reputation faded into obscurity. As a writer he was just not a strong finisher. He started many literary projects—including novels and stories—yet completed few.

In 1950, in the light of renewed anticommunist witch-hunting in the U.S. Congress and the media, Gold moved to France with his wife Elizabeth and their two sons. Poverty was again his lot. In 1957 he returned to the United States, settling in San Francisco for the remainder of his life. There he again wrote for the *Daily Worker* as well as for *People's World,* in which he serialized a continuation of *Jews without Money* that was not well received. Today students of American radicalism still read his *Daily Worker* column "Change the World," which ran for thirty-two years.

For most of his life Gold promoted his idealized image of the working classes by wearing unpressed and often unwashed clothes over an unclean body, using rough language, and living a spartan existence, preferring to be called plain, proletarian-sounding Mike

Gold. Despite the passing of generations, Gold's Whitmanesque image lingers on; today he is more admired and appreciated than he ever was in his lifetime.

In none of his writings did Gold ever clearly distinguish between autobiography and fiction. Thus it is best to label *Jews without Money* a semifictional novel. Of course, it is largely based on his own childhood experiences growing up on Chrystie Street. It remains one of the great documents on family life in the Lower East Side ghetto at the beginning of the twentieth century. At the same time, *Jews without Money* is a powerfully effective, vivid, antibourgeois depiction of the sufferings of the impoverished working class, crying out for social justice for the poor in American society.

Jews without Money is a modernist work in that it employs an urban dialect in a way unlike James Joyce's use of a Dublin dialect in *Portrait of the Artist as a Young Man* and *Ulysses*. Gold's diction reflects a dense, brutal, muscular, even caustic oral expression—an echo of the roaring streets of the Lower East Side. It is rich in imagery, both literal and figurative. It trumpets rebellion in its disrespect for authority, decorum, and convention. Even to today's readers it may prove shocking. The plot is episodic but otherwise unstructured, with a carnivalesque narrative filled with grotesqueries, sexuality, and pain.

Gold's Lower East Side reflects a mingling of various communities: male teenage gangs banding together for self-protection on the streets; a sisterhood of housewives and whores, Jewish and gentile, helping each other survive the oppression of men; a gypsy enclave; workers battling bosses; and religious, Old World Jews struggling to preserve a fast-eroding culture.

The hero of *Jews without Money* is Mikey, a Jewish boy living on Chrystie Street at the beginning of the twentieth century. He is a member of a gang of boys—Mikey, Nigger, Jake, Joey, Abie, Izzy, Harry, Stinker, and Pishteppel—who steal fruit from poor peddlers, use dead cats as missiles to be thrown at their enemies, taunt prostitutes, beat up strangers on their street, and enjoy their summer swims in the filthy East River. His best friend is the contumacious Nigger, a dark-complexioned, tough Jewish kid who, driven by poverty and injustice, becomes a gangster after defeating the rapist/thug

Louis One-Eye. Gold spares no ethnic or racial group from his stereotypical portrayal, nor does he mitigate the slurs and taunts of the street: kike, yid, wop, mick, among many others. Contumely is the standard exchange between ethnic groups. Gold's Lower East Side is neither melting pot nor mosaic but rather a fierce ethnic and racial battleground.

Gold envisioned Mikey as an all-American boy, a Huckleberry Finn under gaslight. Nigger, Mikey's Jim, teaches him about sex and revenges him by banging a schoolteacher on the nose when she calls Mikey a little kike. Mikey and Nigger are the new American inner-city youths—tough, clever, street fighters on the make. The city is the Wild West for the children of Eastern European Jewish immigrants, with the Indians represented by the Irish and Italian gangs that must be fought off.

The vivid cast of characters includes pimps, boxers, coke fiends, pedophiles, corrupt and brutal Irish cops, prostitutes, rabbis, cruel Hebrew teachers, gangsters, unscrupulous politicians, sympathetic doctors, Irish immigrant neighbors, children, and poor Jewish women and men.

Gold foregrounds sex in his portrayal of the ghetto. It is widely for sale. Young male and female children are at risk from pedophiles. Women are used and abused. Gang rape and forced prostitution are common. Boys are able to witness men fornicating with prostitutes. Women are also sexually harassed by factory owners and supervisors.

The backyard of Mikey's tenement was once a small cemetery; the headstones now line the yard. The boys dig up the graves of those early New York City settlers and cart off their bones for their collections. Gold is saying that New York belongs to the young, who have no respect for nor need of the past. The past is always an impediment to the generation on the rise.

Mikey's father, Herman, is a hardworking house painter who regularly becomes ill from the fumes; the lead-filled paint is ruining his lungs and poisoning his stomach. Herman and Mikey are close. The father is proud of his bright son. He takes pleasure in telling Mikey about the adventures he experienced in coming to America. He hopes that Mikey will become a doctor, but in America Jews without money can't send their children to medical school.

When Herman's scaffold falls and his feet are smashed, he is unable to work at his trade. Returning to work after a year convalescing, he can't face the scaffold, so he slowly turns into a pitiful peddler. Herman had bought into the American dream of prosperity and happiness for all. Now a single accident has destroyed his hopes and his confidence. He comes to understand that his son also cannot escape the grinding poverty of the ghetto on his own.

Mikey's strong, loving mother, Katie, becomes the breadwinner, working in a cafeteria when her husband is incapacitated. She can even take on the hated landlord. Gold draws her in the sentimental, venerable tradition of the self-sacrificing, loving, tough, pious, Jewish ghetto mother—a stereotypical characterization embraced by Anzia Yezierska, Henry Roth, and many other Jewish American writers. This adoration—particularly in male Jewish writers—seems to be accompanied by a degree of authorial guilt, as if the classic Oedipal complex were a universal problem among Jewish men.

Katie is cook, baker, cleaner, sage, and nurse all rolled into one. In a pinch she can perform the duties of a midwife for a neighbor. She loves her family to the extent that she would die for them, but she scolds them continually. Katie teaches Mikey about God. He prays for a Jewish Messiah who will look like Buffalo Bill and will smite the hateful gentiles. For Mikey the Messiah is as good as Santa Claus, maybe better.

Mikey's younger sister, Esther, with whom he often fights, takes over the housekeeping chores when Katie goes to work in the cafeteria. One snowy winter day, leaving the flat to look for wood for the stove, she is accidentally struck down by an Adams Express wagon (Gold worked for this company as a boy). She falls between the horses, the heavy wheels run over her, and she dies in the hospital. The family is overwhelmed with grief. There seems no end to their troubles. Katie is devastated. All she can do is cling to Mikey and his little brother.

Herman is unable to feed the family on his meager earnings from selling bananas. Mikey must go out and work. He joins the workforce at the age of twelve. Factory work is brutal. One day Mikey hears an East Side soapbox orator speak passionately of socialism and he decides to join the workers' revolution. Fortunately Gold does not turn the novel into a vehicle for communist propaganda. The doctrinaire revolutionary cant only appears in a dozen or so lines at the end of the text, where Gold elevates the workers' revolution to the status of a messianic religion.

Jews without Money is an aesthetically significant, unified, naturalistic narrative. It depicts generational conflicts, cultural clashes, political strife, and family tragedy that affects the inner-city poor more than any other social class. Alone among Gold's writings—poems, plays, journalism—it has achieved a permanent place in America literature.

Additional Reading

Folsom, Michael, ed. *Mike Gold: A Literary Anthology.* New York: International 1972.
Gold, Michael. *Jews without Money.* Reprint, New York: Carroll and Graf, 1984.

Samson Raphaelson

1896–1983

When he was an undergraduate at the University of Illinois, Samson Raphaelson, who was later to become a celebrated playwright and screenwriter, saw a road-show performance of a musical play that later inspired him to write a short story. The story was adapted into a successful Broadway musical play, which in turn became one of the most important films in the history of the cinema. The musical Raphaelson saw was *Robinson Crusoe Jr.,* which starred the great performer Al Jolson. The title of the story Raphaelson wrote was "The Day of Atonement," which was published in the January 1922 issue of *Everybody's Magazine.* The Broadway musical play was *The Jazz Singer* (1925). The film version, also called *The Jazz Singer* (1927), featured Al Jolson and is credited as the first movie with spoken dialogue.

Samson Raphaelson was born on the Lower East Side and lived there with his grandparents until age eleven, when his parents brought him to live with them in Chicago. After attending high school for two years, he took a variety of jobs and also sold short stories to earn enough money to pay for his college tuition. He was awarded the bachelor of arts degree from the University of Illinois in 1917. After working in advertising in Chicago and New York, and following a brief stint as a *New York Times* reporter, Raphaelson achieved Broadway success with *The Jazz Singer* and decided to write on a full-time basis for the stage and screen. In 1927 Raphaelson married Dorothy Wegman, a Ziegfeld Follies beauty. Two children resulted from their long and happy marriage.

When the undergraduate Raphaelson saw Jolson perform in Champaign, Illinois, on 25 April 1917, he immediately felt that Al Jolson sang with all the passion of a cantor. Raphaelson knew that Jolson's father had been a cantor on the Lower East Side. When, at the beginning of his writing career, he began to write short stories, he imagined a conflict between a religious father and a secular son over the proper use of an inherited talent.

"The Day of Atonement" tells the story of Jakie Rabinowitz, a sensitive Lower East Side Jewish boy who breaks the code of his gang by choosing not to respond to the taunts of an Irish boy from a rival gang. He pays for his refusal to redress an insult to his Jewishness by fighting a member of his own Jewish gang and is beaten. In his fury, he spews the anti-Semitic words onto his Jewish tormentor that were first used on him by his Irish adversary. At home his father, the cantor of the Hester Street Synagogue, beats him when Jakie says he does not want to be a cantor. Even his Hebrew school teacher beats him. Again and again, representations of male childhood on the Lower East Side by male Jewish writers depict a Hobbesian world.

Jakie's father finally relents a little. In a compromise solution, Jakie agrees to sing in the synagogue on the Sabbath and High Holy Days while working as a ragtime singer in music halls on other days. However, he soon neglects the synagogue and his father winds up throwing him out of his house.

On his own, Jakie Rabinowitz—now known as Jack Robin—is building up a successful musical career when he suddenly falls in love with Amy Prentiss, a gentile dancer, whose father is a successful Anglo-Saxon Boston lawyer. Fearing rejection because of his religion, Jack does not tell her about his family. His anguish affects his performance, as does the alcohol he imbibes. After many months, with encouragement from Amy, Jack speaks his heart and she states her love for him. They become engaged and decide to marry. When he tells his parents, they are appalled that he wishes to marry a gentile.

With the approach of Yom Kippur, the Day of Atonement, Jack's mother wants him to attend the services that his father will be conducting. He can't because his Broadway show is opening that evening. Suddenly, a few hours before Yom Kippur commences, his father dies. His last request to his wife is to get Jack to sing during the service. Jack forsakes his Broadway show to carry out his father's last wish. The story ends with the show's producer coming down to the Lower East Side, where he hears Jack sing the following day's service and realizes that Jack Robin will become the greatest ragtime singer in the country.

Raphaelson made some changes in his stage version, now called *The Jazz Singer*. The film company Warner Brothers made others that displeased Raphaelson, including having Jack's father remain alive until he hears his son sing in the synagogue, plus a final scene where Al Jolson, in grotesque blackface, sings an Oedipal love song to his smiling mother, who is sitting in a theater audience with Amy at her side.

What Raphaelson may not have realized in 1927 was that the musical play and the film exposed to millions of Americans a major theme in Jewish American literature and life, namely, the pain and suffering inflicted on an older generation of Orthodox Jews as a result of the inevitable conflict between parents and their American-educated children and grandchildren, who often followed the path of assimilation into the gentile community. That was surely a major achievement. In 1998, while I was lecturing on Lower East Side life at a Jewish temple in La Jolla, California, the seminar's participants were amazed that the 1927 film foregrounded a theme that seemed so parochially Jewish. Two later film versions of Raphaelson's story and another musical continue to underscore the significance of the archetypal theme of rejection and acceptance between generations.

Besides the stage production of *The Jazz Singer*, Raphaelson's most successful plays include: *Young Love* (1928), *Jason* (1942), *The Perfect Marriage* (1945), and *Hilda Crane* (1951), the latter a critically admired domestic drama. Of Raphaelson's many screenplays, Alfred Hitchcock's *Suspicion* (co-screenwriter, 1941) and Ernst Lubitsch's *Shop Around the Corner* (1940) and *Heaven Can Wait* (1943) are his most notable achievements in this medium. Raphaelson also published a novel, *Skylark* (1939), which in play form was produced the same year. He also wrote a practical playwriting text called *The Human Nature of Playwriting* (1949). Reflecting his dual career, Raphaelson was a member of both the Dramatists Guild and the Screenwriters Guild.

Additional Reading

Carringer, Robert L., ed. *The Jazz Singer*. Madison: University of Wisconsin Press, 1979.

Marya Zaturenska

1902–1982

Born Marya Zaturensky in Kiev, then part of Russian Ukraine, as an adolescent living in America she changed her surname to Zaturenska, probably because it sounded Russian rather than Jewish to gentile ears. For most of her adult life she hid her Jewish heritage. Nevertheless, Zaturenska was the most important female poet to emerge from the Lower East Side. Her only competitor for that title is Anna Margolin (1887–1952), but Margolin wrote exclusively in Yiddish and, despite translations, her poetic art is all but forgotten except for the few remaining Yiddish speakers who actually read poetry.

Zaturenska arrived in New York City with her parents circa 1910. She learned English in the public schools and, later, in night high school while working during the day in clothing factories. With improved English skills, she managed to find employment as a salesperson in a bookstore. Later she also worked as a journalist. Zaturenska began to publish poetry as a teenager.

Thanks to her poetry she received a scholarship to Valparaiso University in Indiana. Another followed at the University of Wisconsin. In 1925 she was awarded a degree in library science, held a job as a librarian and, most significantly, married the poet Horace Gregory. Zaturenska and Gregory became one of the few poet-critic married couples in American literary history. The Gregorys had two children.

Zaturenska's first book of poetry, *Threshold and Hearth* (1934), showed that she had a genuine gift for lyric poetry, although her fantasy-filled verse seemed far removed from contemporary diction and events. It was as if she had tried too hard to imitate the techniques, imagery, and subjects of late-nineteenth-century English poetry. It is no coincidence that she wrote an admiring and well-received biography of Christina Rossetti (1949). Zaturenska's other collections of poetry include: *Cold Morning Sky* (1937), *The Listening Landscape* (1941), *The Golden Mirror* (1944), *Terraces of Light* (1960), and *The Hidden Waterfall* (1974). Her *Selected Poems* was published in 1954 and *Collected Poems* in 1965. Zaturenska was also a critic, editor, and biographer. In 1938, at the height of her career, she received the Pulitzer Prize for poetry for *Cold Morning Sky*.

Zaturenska was a deracinated woman who never drew on her own rich cultural heritage to give her poetry authenticity. She sought agency as a writer and a woman through assimilation. If she had been truer to herself, perhaps she would have fulfilled more of her substantial artistic potential and her poems would have had greater contemporary relevance. Nevertheless, Zaturenska wrote some poems of exquisite and polished beauty.

Additional Reading

Zaturenska, Marya. *The Diaries of Marya Zaturenska, 1938–1944.* Syracuse, N.Y.: Syracuse University Press, 2001.
———. *New Selected Poems.* Syracuse, N.Y.: Syracuse University Press, 2002.

Louis Zukofsky

1904–1978

Louis Zukofsky was the most significant American poet to emerge from the Lower East Side. His critical reputation has surpassed that of Marya Zaturenska. Unlike the latter, Zukofsky knew that to be born Jewish is to belong to a club from which there is no resigning and made no attempt to hide his Jewishness. In fact, he held a life-long intellectual interest in and identified with the great Jewish philosopher Spinoza.

Zukofsky's parents, Maisha Afroim and Chana Pruss, Orthodox Jewish agricultural workers with very little education, were born on the outskirts of Must, a small town in Lithuania, then part of the Russian Empire. Three children were born in Europe before they decided to join the Jewish tide and come to America, where, in 1904, Louis was born in a Chrystie Street tenement on the Lower East Side. His father worked as a presser in a garment factory, while his mother attended to the family. Initially all spoke Yiddish exclusively. Louis learned English in New York's public schools, starting with Public School 7 on Chrystie and Hester Streets.

It quickly became apparent to Louis's teachers that he was an intellectually superior child. He was reading Shakespeare at the age of eleven. In high school he began to write poetry. Before his sixteenth birthday he matriculated at Columbia University where he studied literature under Mark Van Doren and philosophy under John Dewey.

After earning a bachelor of arts degree and a master of arts degree at Columbia, Zukofsky taught English literature at the University of

Wisconsin, at Queens College of the City University of New York, and then at Colgate University in Hamilton, New York. Next he worked as an editor in New York City. In 1936 Zukofsky married Celia Thaew, a musician and poet. (The composer and violinist Mark Zukofsky is their son.) As the Great Depression dragged on, Zukofsky wrote for WPA projects until 1947, when he accepted a teaching position at the Polytechnic Institute of Brooklyn, where he taught literature and writing until retiring in 1966.

Zukofsky began publishing his poetry in 1920, and by 1930 he was recognized as a talented new poet whose technique fit in with the reigning modernist style, particularly that of the Objectivists, an offshoot of the more popular Imagists. Fellow Objectivists included William Carlos Williams and Kenneth Rexroth. Williams, who initially claimed that he found Zukofsky's work obscure, later became his friend and admirer.

Surprisingly, the anti-Semitic fascist poet Ezra Pound also admired Zukofsky's work. Zukofsky actually visited Pound in Italy, and Pound's *Cantos* served as a model for Zukofsky's long poems. It was Pound who convinced Harriet Monroe, editor of the influential magazine *Poetry,* to devote an issue to Zukofsky and the other Objectivists. Subsequently Zukofsky influenced the development of such Beat poets as Robert Creeley, Robert Duncan, Charles Olson, and Charles Tomlinson. He in effect became the poet's poet.

Zukofsky was a modernist poet. His work is purposefully ambiguous, resistant, obscurant, punning, deceptively simple-seeming, and nonrepresentational. His great lifelong work *"A,"* begun in 1928 and not completed until 1979, runs to over eight hundred pages of poetry and is a treasure-house of modern American verse. It contains Zukofsky's version of Marxist economics, philosophy, literary criticism, history, snatches of conversation (with the likes of T. S. Eliot), and family history. Zukofsky did not exclude his background and his parents' lives from his poetry. In fact, his mother is central to his early poetry.

The nearest magnum opus to *"A"* in American Literature is *Leaves of Grass* by Brooklyn's own Walt Whitman, an earlier New York City writer. Like *Leaves of Grass, "A"* is an evolving work encompassing a lifetime.

All: The Collected Short Poems, 1923–1958 was published in 1965. *All: The Collected Short Poems, 1956–1964* appeared in 1966. Zukofsky's reputation as a major American modernist poet continues to grow.

Additional Reading

Comens, Bruce. *Apocalypse and After: Modern Strategy and Postmodern Tactics in Pound, Williams, and Zukofsky.* Tuscaloosa: University of Alabama Press, 1995.

Scroggins, Mark. *Louis Zukofsky and the Poetry of Knowledge.* Tuscaloosa: University of Alabama Press, 1998.

Terrell, Carol F., ed. *Louis Zukofsky: Man and Poet.* Orono, Me.: National Poetry Foundation, 1979.

Zukofsky, Louis. *"A": The Complete Poem.* New York: Grossman, 1978.

———. *All: The Collected Short Poems, 1923–1958.* New York: Norton, 1965.

———. *All: The Collected Short Poems, 1956–1964.* New York: Norton, 1966.

———. *Autobiography* (with Celia Zukofsky). New York: Grossman, 1970.

Sydney Taylor

1904–1978

From 1951 to the end of her life Sydney Taylor, the Louisa May Alcott of Jewish American writers, published five children's books that provided two generations of American Jews and gentiles with an idealized picture of early-twentieth-century Jewish family life in New York City. Her books focused on mothers and daughters. Initially she created her fictional *All-of-a-Kind Family* based on the bedtime stories she told her daughter, Jo (named after Jo March in *Little Women*?). They were a way of informing her little girl of her own childhood on the Lower East Side as part of an Orthodox Jewish family. Moreover, she wished to inculcate the traditional Jewish family values of love, respect, compassion, and justice in her only child.

Sydney Taylor (her maiden name was Brenner) was born on the Lower East Side to immigrant parents. She was one of five sisters who grew up in the same tenement-flat bedroom. A little brother came last. After graduating from high school, she studied drama at New York University, acted with the Lennox Hill Players in the 1920s, and danced with the Martha Graham Dance Company in the 1930s. In 1925 she married Robert Taylor, a successful businessman who became president of the Caswell-Massey Company. It was he who submitted his wife's manuscript of *All-of-a-Kind Family* to a publisher. The book received the 1952 Jewish Book Council's award for children's fiction. Taylor had launched what became an outstanding career of writing books for children.

The five *All-of-a-Kind Family* books include: *All-of-a-Kind Family* (1951), *More All-of-a-Kind Family* (1954), *All-of-a-Kind Family*

Uptown (1958), *All-of-a-Kind Family Downtown* (1972), and *Ella of All-of-a-Kind Family* (1978). Taylor also wrote the following: *Mr. Barney's Beard* (1961), *Now That You Are Eight* (1963), *A Papa like Everyone Else* (1966), *The Dog Who Came to Dinner* (1966), and *Danny Loves a Holiday* (1980).

The original *All-of-a-Kind Family* relates the story of an Orthodox Jewish family residing on the Lower East Side in 1912. They live in a typical tenement apartment. The mother and father have five daughters—Ella, Charlotte, Henny, Sarah, and Gertie—ranging in age from twelve to four. In the last chapter the long-awaited son, Charlie, is born. Although they are poor, their life is rich in terms of filial affection, tradition, and contact with the seemingly exotic Lower East Side, where going to the public library or shopping for food with mama is an adventure in itself. The girls are mischievous and fun-loving. The book's atmosphere is as warm as a snuggle in a Jewish mama's bosom.

Although written fourth, *All-of-a-Kind Family Downtown* fits into the family saga as a Lower East Side sequel to *All-of-a-Kind Family.* Taylor branches out culturally by introducing a poor Italian immigrant boy, Guido, who is caring for his ill mother. Taylor is well aware that in the early years of the twentieth century many Italian and Jewish families lived side by side on the Lower East Side. Taylor also introduces the character of a settlement house worker, represented by Miss Carey.

More All-of-a-Kind Family is just that. Naturally, the girls are growing up and rebelling against parental restrictions. Frisky Henny battles with papa over them. The main event involves Charlie getting lost. A kind woman finds him and Uncle Hiram marries her—clearly a sign of deep gratitude. Ella, the oldest, has an East Side boyfriend named Jules.

In a geographical sense *All-of-a-Kind Family Uptown* completes the immigrant journey: from Europe to the Lower East Side and then out of the ghetto. The family moves to the Bronx. The sisters, advancing in age, now begin to understand that growing up means standing tall in the larger American world. In 1917 Ella's boyfriend enlists in the Army as America enters World War I. Along with the family the reader experiences New York City at war.

Ella of All-of-a-Kind Family finds Ella hoping to launch a career in Broadway musicals. She is discovered by a talent scout, and it looks like she will have a life in the theater, but she is still in love with Jules, who is returning from the front. She must choose between him and a stage career. With the help of the family she makes the "right" choice of marriage. Family values triumph again and again in the *All-of-a-Kind* series.

Sydney Taylor's children's books sanitized and idealized the hard life of immigrant families living on the Lower East Side and the less difficult life of those Jewish people who had moved uptown to the Bronx or across the East River to Brooklyn. Her model Jewish family is very traditional: papa works; mama rules the home from her headquarters in the kitchen; the sisters are subordinated when a son arrives; and Ella, the heroine of the last *All-of-a-Kind Family* novel, chooses to raise a family rather than pursue a career!

By presenting the Lower East Side as the new "old country" of American Jews, Taylor helped create the current nostalgia for the former Jewish ghetto of New York City. Perhaps inadvertently, she gave American Jews a wellspring of memory, a saga involving overcoming great adversity and surviving seemingly intact, and a sense of identity they could be proud of. The prestigious Sydney Taylor Body-of-Work Award was established by the Association of Jewish Libraries in 1979.

Additional Reading

Taylor, Sydney. *All-of-a-Kind Family.* Reprint, Magnolia, Mass.: Peter Smith, 1989.
———. *All-of-a-Kind Family Downtown.* Reprint, New York: Dell, 1989.
———. *All-of-a-Kind Family Uptown.* Reprint, New York: Dell, 1983.
———. *Ella of All-of-a-Kind Family.* Reprint, New York: Taylor Productions, 1988.
———. *More All-of-a-Kind Family.* Reprint, New York: Dell, 1989.

Henry Roth

1906–1995

Henry Roth's *Call It Sleep,* a modernist, stream-of-consciousness novel, is America's answer to James Joyce's *Portrait of the Artist as a Young Man*. First published in 1934, *Call It Sleep* is the greatest of the early Jewish American novels. This semiautobiographical tale of a child's life on the Lower East Side at the beginning of the twentieth century is one of the most truthful and poignant depictions of the terrors of childhood ever written. Although Roth wrote short stories and, after a long hiatus, a tetralogy of novels with the collective title *Mercy of a Rude Stream* (1994–98; the last two volumes were published posthumously), it is on *Call It Sleep* that his literary reputation rests.

Henry Roth was born in Tysmenica, in what was then the province of Galicia within the Austro-Hungarian Empire and is now in Ukraine. His parents and grandparents were Orthodox Jews. Shortly after Roth's birth, his father, Herman Roth, a waiter, left him and his mother, Leah Farb, at home while he sailed to New York City to find work and secure a new home for his family. When Henry Roth was about eighteen months old, his mother crossed the Atlantic and arrived at Ellis Island, where his father met and brought them to a tenement flat in the Brownsville section of Brooklyn. The Roths lived in Brooklyn only briefly. In 1910 they moved to a tenement on East Ninth Street on the Lower East Side. Roth's sister, Rose, was born there.

In 1914 the Roth family moved again, this time to East 119th Street in Harlem in order to live near grandparents and other relatives.

Eight-year-old Henry now continued the education he had commenced on the Lower East Side in a community that was primarily Irish and Italian. The security he had felt in the more homogeneous community of the Lower East Side gave way to insecurity in close contact with anti-Semitic gentiles and their children. One result of the move was the weakening of the boy's faith in the religion of his parents, which was probably a partial cause of Roth's later atheism.

Roth's parents quarreled a great deal. Herman bullied his wife and son. As a child Roth disliked his father immensely and loved his mother inordinately. His father came to symbolize the brutality, violence, and terror in the child's world, while his mother symbolized beauty, grace, kindness, and protectiveness.

After elementary school the bright youth studied at Stuyvesant High School and De Witt Clinton High School. In 1924 he entered City College of New York. He published his first short story, "Impressions of a Plumber," in *Lavender,* the City College literary magazine. In 1927 Roth met the person who would serve as a mentor and guide him toward serious authorship: Eda Lou Walton, a poet from New Mexico who was teaching literature at New York University in Greenwich Village. Despite the fact that she was twelve years older than Roth, they became lovers and she introduced him to the Greenwich Village radicals, writers, artists, and theater people that comprised the American literary avant-garde of the time. When, in 1928, Roth moved in with Walton and shared her Greenwich Village residence on Morton Street, he was close enough to walk to the Lower East Side street of his formative childhood years. Shortly afterward he began to write about those agonizing, traumatic years—primarily because he did not want to forget them. Surely Gold's then recently published semiautobiographical novel *Jews without Money* was on his mind.

Roth and Walton lived together for ten years. She supported him financially and emotionally while he wrote. She was like a substitute mother. Through Walton Roth met such literary luminaries as Hart Crane, Mark Van Doren, and Louise Bogan. In 1930 Roth accompanied Walton to her residency at the Yaddo writers' colony. He lived in a hotel, writing, while she worked and fraternized with other creative residents. Walton believed in Roth's talent. She gave Roth confidence as a writer, introduced him to modernist writing through T. S. Eliot's *The Waste Land* and James Joyce's *Portrait* and *Ulysses,* and encouraged his work on *Call It Sleep.* Initially Roth began to write an autobiography, but he quickly changed to a modern bildungsroman, part expressionistic and part naturalistic. In 1934, after four years of effort, the book was published by Robert Ballou, thanks to a subsidy by Walton's friend David Mandel. Roth dedicated the novel to Walton.

Roth never thought he had written a proletarian novel like Gold's *Jews without Money,* but since he professed to be a Marxist—he had joined the Communist Party in 1933, perhaps feeling guilty over being a kept man when other men were standing on bread lines— the radical press had expected a revolution-inspired text and was perplexed and angered. Other critics did not as yet understand the parameters of a psychological stream-of-conscious novel.

Less biased and more perceptive critics recognized the book's original and powerful use of language and its structural solidity. In the end the novel made only a slight impression on the literary scene. The fact that *Call It Sleep* came out at the height of the Depression and that the publisher went bankrupt soon after its publication did not help. But it did impress the leading book editor of the time, Scribner's Maxwell Perkins, who in 1936 gave Roth an advance on a second novel about an injured factory worker who becomes a communist and a labor organizer. Doing research on the New York waterfront one day, he was jumped and beaten by a pack of union thugs. Discouraged with American society during the Depression era, Roth never finished the nearly completed novel.

Roth tried to start a narrative about his adolescence, but his inability to write a proletarian novel that matched his political convictions seemed to have caused a near total writer's block for many years—indeed, there was a hiatus of fifty years between novels that ended in a veritable tsunami of words, namely, the four volumes of *Mercy of a Rude Stream* (1994–98). Meanwhile *Call It Sleep* had faded from the public's collective memory and awaited resurrection.

Finally attaining a belated sense of maturity in 1939, a year after separating from Walton, Roth married Muriel Parker, a composer, whom he had met at Yaddo. While still writing a few short stories, from 1939 to 1941 Roth taught English classes in night school at

Theodore Roosevelt High School in the Bronx. *The New Yorker* published "Broker" and "Somebody Always Grabs the Purple" in 1939. That year Roth became disillusioned with the American Communist Party when it supported the German-Russian nonaggression pact.

During World War II Roth performed war work as a precision tool grinder in New York, Boston, and Providence, Rhode Island. Henry and Muriel's two sons, Jeremy and Hugh, were born during the war. With the war over, the Roths decided to leave hectic urban life and move to a more rural locale outside of Center Montville, Maine.

Roth did what he could to support his family, such as teaching in a one-room schoolhouse and fighting fires for the Forestry Service. In 1949 they bought a tiny farm near Augusta, Maine. Roth worked as an attendant at Maine State Hospital until 1949, when he left his job and he and Muriel earned a livelihood raising ducks and geese. Roth also tutored pupils in various high-school subjects. Muriel took up teaching as well and eventually became an elementary-school principal.

In Maine Roth had basically quit writing, although *The New Yorker* published one story in 1956 and *Commentary* published two autobiographical pieces in 1959 and 1960. Then something miraculous happened. In 1956 the editors of *The American Scholar* asked some literary critics, scholars, and historians to indicate their choice of the most undeservedly neglected book of the past twenty-five years. Two leading Jewish intellectuals, Leslie Fiedler and Alfred Kazin, picked *Call It Sleep.* In 1960 Pageant Books reissued Roth's novel. It stirred up an unexpected degree of interest. Consequently a mass-market publisher, Avon Press, brought out a paperback edition. Thanks to a rave review by Jewish critic and intellectual Irving Howe in the *New York Times Book Review* (25 October 1964), *Call It Sleep* became an international best-seller. Roth was suddenly elevated to the status of a major twentieth-century American writer. Simultaneously with the resurrection of Roth and his novel, a growing interest in the immigrant Jewish experience on the Lower East Side led to the reissuance of the fiction of other major Lower East Side writers like Abraham Cahan and Anzia Yezierska.

In 1965 Roth was awarded a grant from the National Institute of Arts and Letters, which he used to pay for trips to Mexico and Spain.

In 1967 Roth broke with communism when the Soviet Union supported the Arabs during the Six-Day War. Feeling that he had somehow experienced a rebirth as he returned to Judaism, in the late 1960s and 1970s Roth visited Israel and contemplated emigration, ultimately deciding against it on the grounds of unfamiliarity with the language and the culture.

In 1968, after being awarded a D. H. Lawrence Fellowship from the University of New Mexico, and following Muriel Roth's retirement from her teaching job in Maine, Henry and Muriel moved to Albuquerque, New Mexico. Roth had enjoyed and been inspired by a stay at D. H. Lawrence's ranch at Taos, where he was writer-in-residence. Roth began to work on *Mercy of a Rude Stream,* his massive series of novels based on his life following his childhood on the Lower East Side.

In 1987 *Shifting Landscape*—a collection of Roth's short stories, articles, and interviews—was published. Muriel died in 1990 and Roth continued to work on the volumes of *Mercy of a Rude Stream* until his death in 1995. Four have been published, while two remain unpublished.

Call It Sleep, a novel gratifyingly full of hermeneutic challenges, is the story of David Schearl's (the biblical name David means "beloved" in Hebrew) early childhood, beginning at the age of two in the prologue and then spanning ages six through eight in the main text. Almost the entire book is written from David's point of view. It is a child's-eye view. What Roth strives for and succeeds in accomplishing is to have the reader identify intimately with the inner and outer world of a specific child. David is an extremely sensitive, Oedipal, Jewish boy who at age two is taken from his native Poland and thrust into the terrifying worlds of working-class Brownsville and the Lower East Side. "Schearl" means scissors in Yiddish, implying that David's father, the jealous Albert Schearl, is psychologically trying to castrate his rival. But the name is shared by David, where it symbolizes his need to cut himself off from the power of his father and, perhaps, the smothering love of his mother, Genya, in order to achieve selfhood. Lastly, David will also cut himself off from his religion.

Structurally the novel consists of the "Prologue" and four parts: "The Cellar," "The Coal," "The Picture," and "The Rail." In the

"Prologue" the year is 1907 and the reader joins onlookers observing the reunion of an immigrant family at Ellis Island. Albert Schearl, there to meet his wife, Genya, and only child, David, is clearly displeased with them. His rude behavior produces a cold welcome, indicating that something is clearly amiss in the relationship between wife and husband. Schearl takes his displeasure out on their hapless son. Later it becomes clear that Albert wrongly suspects that the boy is not his biological child. It is true that prior to marrying Albert Genya had an affair with a gentile who abandoned her, but David is Albert's son. It is already obvious to the reader that David is to be subjected to the extremes of his paranoid father's hatred and his mother's smothering love.

In "The Cellar" David is approaching his sixth birthday. The cellar represents the id, the child's deepest needs and fears and the root source of David's emotional development. It is the first place outside of the womblike apartment he must pass in order to reach the street. The door of the cellar bulges as if something monstrous is trying to escape and catch him. The cellar, which must be encountered and dealt with on a daily basis and whose contents are unknown, terrifies David and seems to bar access to the freedom represented by the street.

In this section David comes to sense that his father's "friend" Luter threatens his relationship with his mother and the fragile stability of the Schearl family. His subconscious mind senses the power and the danger of sex. When he finds himself looking at his mother's cleavage the way Luter did, he purges himself of the thought of what pleasure or comfort lies in the dark space between Genya's breasts.

David's friend Yussie Mink shows him a rat trap and describes in detail how it works. When the disgusted David learns that the rats emerge from the cellar, he is doubly terrified of the place. Yussie's sister, Annie, takes David into a closet to play "bad," and after explaining in gross terms how babies are made, she puts his hand on her genitals and offers to touch his. David is not ready for this and he resists. It seems that all the dangerous places are areas of dark confinement. The sight of a black coffin with a dead man inside racks him with fear. His mother's calm explanation of death slightly assuages his archetypal fear, but David is left with the vision of yet another dark place in his future—the eternal grave.

Distraught upon seeing Luter enter his house when his father is away, and convinced that Luter and Genya are playing the horrid sex game that Annie taught him, David wanders about aimlessly until it is time to return home before his father does, only to find himself lost. Kind people try to help him, but they can't understand his pronunciation of the name of the street he lives on. Taken to a police station, the compassionate cops also try to determine where he lives. His mother is finally contacted, and she brings the exhausted and terrified child, who is still clutching a piece of cake the cops have given him, back home again. Paradoxically, all the adult men he encounters during his frightening ordeal seem gentler to him than his own father.

Luter does not return to have meals with the Schearls, but instead acts guilty at the workplace he shares with Albert, who cannot understand why Luter won't look him in the eye and avoids talking to him. The paranoid Albert, finding his one friendship sour, intends to beat Luter but instead accidentally catches his own finger in a printing press. Wounded, he vows never to work as a printer again. Genya is racked by guilt over Luter's visit and her belief that she has caused the split that resulted in her husband's injury. She also worries that David may know that Luter visited her in the afternoon and could tell Albert, so she is both relieved and saddened that Luter is no longer entangled in their lives.

In "The Picture" the Schearl family has moved from the quiet and sedate Brownsville section of Brooklyn to Ninth Street and Avenue D on the vibrant, teeming Lower East Side. Life is harder. In their tenement they must share a toilet with other families and there is no bathtub. Albert no longer has a day job. As a milkman he must leave for work at night and return early in the morning.

Despite Albert's displeasure, Aunt Bertha, Genya's younger sister, has just arrived from Europe to live with the Schearls. Bertha is gross, foul-mouthed, and ugly, but she is also tough and quite capable of taking Albert on. She is funny too, and one of the few amusing scenes in the narrative takes place when Bertha and David get lost within the Metropolitan Museum of Art. They don't possess the language ability to locate an exit, so they shadow a couple until the unsuspecting pair decide to leave the museum and lead the exhausted aunt and nephew to an exit.

Nevertheless, the depiction of Bertha can only be described as disgusting. Her lust for illicit information about her sister's earlier life and her inability to keep a sister's confidences cause much grief within the Schearl family. The reader senses a touch of anti-Semitism—and even misogyny—in Roth's portrayal of the one strong woman in the narrative.

Ultimately Bertha finds a suitor in Nathan, a garment-industry worker and a widower with two preteen daughters. When Nathan comes to dinner, the vindictive Albert tries to destroy the relationship, but to no avail, for Bertha is a match for any man, including her somewhat mousy suitor. They eventually buy a candy store and live in the back rooms with the two girls.

The central event of "The Picture" occurs when Genya buys a painting from a pushcart seller. It is a landscape depicting a field of corn and blue flowers. Although she says it reminds her of her home in Austria (Austrian Poland), it really helps her to sustain the memory of her happy moments of love in the fields with the gentile who abandoned her. Poor Genya's life with Albert is so miserable that, except for her son David, the only pleasure she has is looking at her picture.

Bertha eventually pries Genya's secret from her. She had a gentile lover, a handsome church organist named Ludwig. He was already engaged to a rich woman with a large dowry. Genya's parents found out about the relationship and her father beat her. Six months later she met Albert, whom she never told about her first love. She was pushed into marriage by her parents. Unfortunately for Genya, David overhears her confession and understands more than she would wish. The picture and her own son will eventually betray her.

"The Coal" finds David, now aged seven, sent to a cheder, an afternoon Hebrew school, a Dickensian place run by a mean and filthy rabbi, Reb Yidel, and attended by wretched boys who do not want to be there. In the cheder David learns that the lips of the prophet Isaiah were touched by a burning coal held in the hands of an angel who got it from God's cellar. That is how Isaiah was able to speak to God. David associates the ability to speak to God with torment, followed by salvation. David also learns that Moses, in pharaoh's palace, saved his own life by choosing coal over gold. Later in the novel David will learn that there is coal in the cellar and that envisioning the coal helps to bring him back to life after he has nearly electrocuted himself.

David proves to be the outstanding pupil in his Hebrew class, but he is unable to ask the rabbi about God. It is Genya who explains that God is power. When three Irish boys jump David, he denies his Jewishness. They show him the power of the electric trolley by making him drop a zinc sword in the channel of the charged rail. The sight of the blue electrical flash transfixes the child, recalling Isaiah and the burning coal. Unwillingly, David has found the source of power that will redeem him at the end of the narrative. He even goes so far as to break into the locked cheder in order to locate the powerful blue book containing the story of Isaiah. David is now a visionary as well as a traumatized child who will hurt many people and himself before he makes peace with his father, thereby resolving the Oedipal impasse and allowing him to have a more normal life.

In "The Rail," the fourth and longest section of *Call It Sleep,* the Oedipal impasse continues as David, having been tormented by his father and taunted by the boys in the cheder, flees home to find his mother wearing a damp, loose-fitting robe after having emerged from a bath in the washtub. The sight of secret parts of her body and the feel of her flesh next to his immediately calms the overwrought child. Shortly afterward, on the street his pals tell him how they peeped in a window and saw a naked woman in a washtub. It was David's mother and he is maddened to tears by the thought of this "violation" of his mother.

Meanwhile, Albert has bought a totem picture for himself and has hung it prominently in the front room of the flat. Depicting a massive bull, it reminds him of the days when he herded his father's cattle and let a bull gore his father to death. The picture also symbolizes Albert's power over his wife. On an even more symbolic level, the bull's horns represents his continual suffering over the thought that he could have been cuckolded by Genya back in Austrian Poland. Ironically, the only possible cuckolding occurred in America with his "friend" Luter. For David the horns on the bull symbolize the threat to his life or his approaching manhood, a threat he knows he must face in the future.

On the roof David sees a boy with a kite on another roof. He has blond hair and blue eyes. David knows that those features don't belong on Ninth Street, which is primarily Jewish. David wants to make friends with the stranger. Like his father, David needs a male friend. Like his mother, David is attracted to the exotic good looks of a gentile. Leo, a twelve-year-old Polish American, is a lucky lad as far as David is concerned because he has roller skates and no father. Leo points to a cross on a building and informs David that the Savior died on such a cross. David is fascinated by the word "Savior." He needs a savior to shield him from his father. Leo also wears a scapular with the Virgin and child painted on it. He tells David that wearing it makes him unafraid. Since David is afraid most of the time, he would like not to be afraid. He can also relate to a picture of Mary adoring her son.

Leo is the first gentile David knows and the first to inform him that Jews killed Christ. David is intrigued by the implied power of the rosary he sees in Leo's apartment and is willing to introduce his friend to his aunt's stepdaughters in exchange for a broken rosary. Leo wants to have sex with the girls. David is so enamored of his gentile older friend—who seems to be freer and have access to the kind of power and surety he longs for—that he will even pimp for Leo.

David receives the promised rosary just before Leo forces himself on twelve-year-old Esther. Ironically, the only "rewards" he receives are a beating from the outraged Esther and the revelation that his "friend" Leo is really another Jew-hater.

Terrified by the encounter with sex and religious hatred, David rushes to the cheder, where he lies to the rabbi in order to mask his distraught state by saying that his mother is dead, that she died long ago, and that the woman who first brought him to the rabbi was really his aunt. He further informs the rabbi that Aunt Bertha, his "other" aunt, had just revealed this "truth" to him. Using the fragment of information he gleaned from eavesdropping on Genya and Bertha, David compounds the lie by telling Reb Yidel that his "real" father was an organist in a church. This, of course, is the kind of information—possibly confirming David's supposed illegitimacy—that would drive Albert insane. David's "confession" is a manifestation of the boy's inward desire to have a different father, to be a Christian like Leo, to be a part of the safer and stronger majority, to possess freedom and power and, lastly, to be able to drop the seemingly unbearable burden of his parents' religion. Now he can do just that, since he has a rosary.

Reb Yidel is perplexed. For next few pages of text the point of view shifts from David to the rabbi. Reb Yidel does not know what to do about David's revelations. After some deliberation he goes to the Schearl residence, where he is met by Genya at the door.

Meanwhile, Esther's sister, Polly, informs her parents of what has happened to Esther. The pregnant Bertha and her husband Nathan fight over who should have been watching the girls. Nathan runs out of the store to inform on David, whom he blames for the attack on his daughter. Bertha tries to stop him before Albert finds out and beats David. It is too late. David faces his parents and the rabbi upon returning home, having wandered in fear of what will happen to him. When the rabbi repeats David's statements, a furious round of revelations and confessions ensues. Genya is terrified because Albert now knows what he has suspected all along, namely, that she had a lover before they were married. Genya was not a pure bride. She was foisted off on him. Albert wrongly believes that Genya was pregnant when they were married, and that her parents purposely "lost" David's birth certificate, which would have indicated an earlier birth than was reported to him.

Genya now lets on that she had heard that Albert allowed his father to be gored to death by a bull, but that she never believed the story. Albert demands to know the identity of David's father. Convinced that Albert is mad, Genya is preparing to take David and leave her husband immediately when Bertha and Nathan suddenly appear. The scene is one of pandemonium. Bertha tries to prevent her husband from informing on David, but before Albert beats the story out of Nathan, David starts to confess and hands his father his horsewhip to punish him. Now Albert is sure that David has done something terrible. When the child reveals all, Albert denies paternity and begins to whip David furiously. The rosary and a cross fall to the floor, further "evidence" to the shocked and amazed group that David is the son of a gentile. Albert is restrained from murdering his son by Bertha and Nathan, while Genya flings open the door and orders David to run for his life.

David runs wildly, hysterically, through the streets. Chancing upon a milk can, he removes the long dipper and runs to the trolley tracks, where he intends to use the dipper as a wand to release the flaming blue power that will purportedly save him.

In order to build suspense, Roth briefly shifts the novel's point of view from David to a description of the Avenue D environment through which a streetcar line cuts. The sounds of a dozen accents pierce the air of the Lower East Side babel. Suddenly people are seen running to the place where a long burst of flame has erupted, where they come upon the seemingly lifeless body of a child that has been electrocuted. David had thrust the handle of the dipper into the crack in the third rail. Symbolically understood, it is a desperate, defiant, phallic act of thrusting and penetration in order to capture or kill at the font of regenerative force.

Using brooms, the people sweep the body away from the rail as if it were trash. The dipper is nearly destroyed. A skeptical policeman tries to resuscitate the boy. An ambulance jangles onto the scene and a medical intern jumps out to help. He applies artificial respiration and discovers that David, although not dead, is barely clinging to life.

As the point of view shifts back to David, the reader learns that inside his mind the child has found the burning coal of Isaiah shining as brightly as a pearl. The resurrected child is borne to his home. His ankle has a second-degree burn, but otherwise he is miraculously unharmed. The family is shocked to see David carried in by a policeman, followed by the young doctor and a crowd. Albert's face is ashen with fear. His mother is screaming in anguish. People are pointing at Albert accusingly and speaking of a deadly quarrel. Questioned by the policeman, Albert admits that David is his eight-year-old son. It is a triumphant moment for David since his father has admitted paternity. Women offer to help Genya make tea, perhaps indicating that she is finally part of a community of women.

Thanks to David's self-sacrificial act, his willingness to assume his mother's penance by immolating himself, the family crisis has passed. The thought of the near tragic death of an only child overwhelms the suspicion, guilt, hatred, and paranoia that has made the Schearl family so dysfunctional.

Albert slinks off to buy medicinal oil, while David is comforted by Genya and urged to sleep. David cannot really sleep, for his mind remains active. He feels neither pain nor terror now. The Oedipal child knows that somehow he has won. Unlike Oedipus, however, he can see clearly at the end.

The portrait of Albert Schearl is a child's nightmare of a father who beats his six-year-old son with a clothes hanger and wishes him dead. Because of Albert, David's wanderings in the dangerous labyrinthine Lower East Side should be seen as an unconscious attempt to escape torture or even death. Both mother and son must huddle together for mutual protection, while existing alongside the monster in their home.

Like D. H. Lawrence's *Sons and Lovers,* another Freudian modernist story of a mother and son bonding against a bestial father almost to the point of unnaturalness, *Call It Sleep* shows no mercy for the tormented male parent. The father in the four-volumes of *Mercy of a Rude Stream* is also a vicious brute. Unlike *Sons and Lovers,* a novel Roth surely read, the more gentle and genteel mother here still has some feeling for her husband, and although Genya had forever lost her heart to her gentile lover, she would care for Albert again and presumably would even make love with him again if he stopped abusing her and their son.

Albert, who hated his father because of his cruelty toward him, let the older man die when he could have saved him. Clearly Albert sees the father-son relationship as a confrontational one. Just as he betrayed his father, so he expects a betrayal from David. The way for the patriarch to save himself from the fate he doled out to his own father is to destroy his son.

Albert, who had trained to become a printer, a reputable trade, drifts from job to job because in his paranoia he sees slights and offense everywhere. He is always seeking vengeance for something. No longer able to find work in the printing trade because of his reputation for anger and violence, he becomes a lowly milkman—truly a comedown for a skilled artisan. Albert Schearl is not only his son's enemy; he is his own enemy as well.

Genya Schearl's is another brilliant characterization. Of course, she is one more saintly Jewish mother ready to do anything to protect her beloved son, but this Jewish mother is imbued with warm sexuality and is devoid of shrewishness. Since she was "damaged goods" as far as her family was concerned, Genya, like Albert and like her son, was cruelly treated by her father. The three main characters in the novel suffered at the hands of the male parent. Paternal abuse appears to be an inherited patriarchal disease, at least in the works of Roth.

The gentle and pretty Genya is courted and pursued by Albert's supposed friend Luter, who correctly surmises that this attractive woman was not having sex with her bullying husband. Genya's relationship with David is Oedipal to a fault, but it is also a portrait of pure, archetypal, instinctive maternal love.

Like so many immigrant Jewish women who came to a country whose language is different from their native one, Genya exists in the prison of her small apartment. Except for shopping trips to the nearby pushcarts and mom-and-pop stores to buy food, she is never outside for long. When she must find her way to a police station to claim David after he has become lost, her journey is a fearful one for her. Ironically, her seven-year-old son has more mobility and travels farther in the neighborhood than she ever did. During the entire course of the narrative—spanning some six years, including the "Prologue"—she has never learned English. Although her opportunities to learn English are severely limited by the prescribed gender roles of wife and mother, she could have done more to acquire some fluency in the language of her adopted country. She is not saddled with roomers. She has only one child. The flat is small. Genya, however, is somewhat indolent and too content in the confines of her home. She has made few if any true friends even though there are dozens of Yiddish-speaking women around her who are living as she does. Her fear of her husband and his bitter, biting tongue may have prevented her from making female friends and inviting them into her home. Only the brief period during which her sister Bertha stayed with her—full of friction though it was—granted her some form of daily adult companionship.

David Schearl, unable to cope with all his problems and fears, needs tranquility. He searches for a power to bring him peace. David is a mystic. He is in search of a faith, a power, a redeemer, even though, as a child, he cannot understand any of the driving motivations of his young life. David is engaged in the archetypal quest for transfiguration. He has his epiphany when he encounters the raw power of the rail. The crowd that comes to the aid of the stricken child thinks he is dead. But he comes back to life. The shock that racks his body energizes David and leaves enough stored power in his little body to give him the drive to endure the tribulations that still await him.

David is revolted by the thought of sex. He has been traumatized by his experience in the closet with Annie, and when he discovers that his mentor Leo has forced himself upon his cousin Esther in Aunt Bertha's cellar, he is again disgusted. The dank, dark cellar symbolizes the vagina, what Annie had called the "knish" into which men put their "pretzel." The toilet or "shit house," as Leo calls it, in cousin Esther's home is in the cellar too. The thought that his mother could have had sex with Albert's "friend" Luter is unbearable to David, for his mother must be like the Christ child's mother, a virgin devoted only to him. In Freudian terms the cellar is the id. It is locked in a titanic struggle with the superego, the imposed, controlling, terrifying will of the father.

David achieves redemption at the novel's end. He has boldly liberated himself from Albert's tyranny. The latter, himself shocked by David's near-fatal execution, realizes how insanely he has acted toward his son. David has achieved the strength of personhood. He has repealed the primal law of the father.

It must also be said of David that although he is very sensitive and intelligent, he is not a likable child. He is a compulsive and skillful liar. Sometimes he seems malevolent in his unerring ability to reveal things that hurt people who care for him. He is so attached to his mother that the reader occasionally feels more sympathy for Albert than for David in their archetypal father-son struggle.

Roth used proper English and poetic translations for the Yiddish speakers, reserving broken English for the occasions when his characters actually speak in English. The English "translation" of Yiddish, as it emerges from the mouths of the characters, is eloquent, while the broken English that is spoken is a crude, dialectical street slang that purposefully grates on the ear. Roth is indicating his belief that there was a cultural loss, perhaps temporary, when the Jewish immigrants slowly abandoned their native language for their new one. In the end, however, Roth chose to write in English, his school-taught language, not Yiddish.

Other languages are represented in this literary babel, such as the Hebrew and Aramaic of the Hebrew Bible, and Polish, which is spoken when Genya reveals to Bertha that she had had a love affair before her marriage. Roth saw the Lower East Side as a place where languages and accents led to confusion, mistaken ideas, and dangerous assumptions. Language foils communication as much as it aids it. Lower East Side life flounders in linguistic anarchy. Roth particularly disliked the spending of endless hours reading Hebrew Scripture in cheder with little or no effort by the instructor to teach the meaning of the words.

Interestingly, David's English improves as he ages. At first his "Yiddish" is good and his English is broken. Halfway through the text his "Yiddish" and English are about equal. Empathizing with David, the reader sequentially experiences the pristine "Yiddish" as his mother speaks, the authentically crude and obscene patois of the street, and the vivid, image-laden monologue of David Schearl's exploration of the landscape of self.

When Roth resumed writing novels some sixty years after *Call It Sleep*, he showed that he had lost the intense Joycean vision that had informed his first novel. *A Star Shines Over Mt. Morris Park* (1994), the first of four autobiographical novels under the collective title *Mercy of a Rude Stream*, continues the saga of the Schearl family, now called the Stigmans. David Schearl is Ira Stigman. The family has just moved from the Lower East Side into the then predominantly Irish neighborhood of Harlem. Ira is eight. Like David Schearl at the end of *Call It Sleep*, the child lives in a borderland of incipient violence between Jewish and gentile groups. The novel ends when Ira is fourteen, in junior high school, and working part time for a fancy food store. Ira is as troubled as David was—Roth's protagonists are always at war with themselves. Ira has difficulty coming to terms with his emerging sexuality. The Oedipal conflict continues, although it seems less interesting.

The strength of the novel lies in Roth's ability to set the scene: the grim life of the urban poor in the expanding economy of early-twentieth-century America, specifically the painful struggle of immigrant Jewish children living outside the Lower East Side ghetto as they face the barriers and the violence of rampant anti-Semitism. Unfortunately, the narrative is not dynamic enough to hold the reader's attention. The explanatory intrusions and commentaries—including a conversation with his computer by the elderly author—halt the flow of the text. As a result, the novel seems more like a series of vignettes than a narrative whole.

A Diving Rock on the Hudson (1995) continues Ira Stigman's journey through life. He is thrown out of prestigious Stuyvesant High School in Manhattan and continues at De Witt Clinton High School in the Bronx. A female New York University professor, the lover of his friend Larry, introduces Ira to New York City's literary world. Central to the novel is the theme of incest. For six years Ira has had sex with his younger sister Minnie, and for a part of that time he has also been intimate with Stella, an even younger cousin.

Despite the usual disclaimer that the novel is a work of fiction, Roth uses the narrative seemingly to confess the sins and crimes of his youth, shameful actions that the author and his dopplegänger, Ira, did pursue. But Roth is a modernist writer, ossified in the time of high modernism. The act of laying bare one's psyche and revealing the degeneration and cruelty in society without privileging one's self is largely what modernist fiction is about. Joyce, Roth's lifelong literary mentor, does not spare his alter-ego Stephen Daedelus in either *Portrait* or *Ulysses*.

The Jewish world depicted in *A Diving Rock on the Hudson* is a sad place, a world without charm, humor, or beauty. Ira's mother possesses neither the attractiveness nor the affection of Genya. Although his father is no Albert, he is still not a person to admire, for he, too, is capable of abusing his family. Other Jews are grasping. The entire community is damned as soulless, without poetry or vision. Ira/Roth is full of Jewish self-hatred. All that is fine and fair belongs to the gentile world that Ira secretly wishes to embrace, but he is held back by the shackles of the "backward" culture he was born into. Ira's rapacious sinning is a manifestation of his self-hatred and his rejection of the moral strictures of his religion. Ira/Roth rejects Judaism itself. Although the novel has many vivid street scenes, for the most part the sky is as uniformly gray as the endless rows of tenements in old Harlem.

From Bondage (1996), published posthumously, has the narrator intervening more and more as he continues to carry on conversations with his computer, seemingly the only companion he has left. Like Krapp's tape recorder in Beckett's *Krapp's Last Tape,* the computer is both listener and capacious storer of the past.

Now well into the 1920s, Ira Stigman speaks a more refined English as his formal education continues and as he comes into contact with people who can engage in discourse on James Joyce and *Ulysses.* Ira is a middling student at City College of New York. He is also working after school at various part-time jobs. His friend Larry's lover, Edith, a New York University professor, takes to Ira and allows him to be her confidante. A three-sided relationship ensues, but Edith, though willing, does not become Ira's mistress in this volume. We are, however, introduced to a girl designated as "M" for whom Ira feels real passion. As a result of these intimacies, coupled with Jewish guilt and self-hatred, and the welling up of emotive experience, it is presumed but not demonstrated that Ira can begin to write seriously.

Requiem for Harlem (1998), posthumously published like *Bondage,* is the fastest paced and most powerfully written of the four volumes of *Mercy of a Rude Stream* currently in print. Set in the late 1920s, it is the story of Ira Stigman's escape from the Harlem neighborhood in which he has grown up. In order to shake off his guilt and his unhappiness with his family, he must leave everything behind. As is always the case in life, he can never fully escape the trauma, pain, suffering, hatred, and fears of childhood, adolescence, and early adulthood.

Mrs. Stigman is impossibly mournful. Mr. Stigman is still a brute. Ira's sexual relationship with his sister, Minnie, must come to an end, and though brother and sister remain friends, Minnie is always a little suspicious of Ira. Cousin Stella terrifies Ira when she reveals to him that she thinks she may be pregnant. Still, he can't keep his hands off her.

The key to his escape is his relationship with Edith, the educated, urbane shiksa. She will lead him out of the Harlem labyrinth. Edith is miserable since she is pregnant with the child of an ex-lover. Because Ira comforts her, in the end he is able to move in with her and they begin their life as a couple, thus completing his escape. In doing so he confesses his sexual exploitation of his sister and cousin, and Edith accepts him despite his history. She is his all-forgiving mother figure. Their "child" will be his first novel. The artist as a young man is ready to create his own identity in life and in art.

Unlike David Schearl, Ira Stigman is never a likable character. He is rapacious, manipulative, twisted, selfish, and disgustingly egotistical. Roth created this character with the full understanding that this was how the reader would feel about the author too. *Mercy of a Rude Stream* is Roth's confession and penance for the sins of his youth.

Obviously, *Mercy of a Rude Stream* could never recapture the youthful passions, pain-charged sensibilities, and acute vision of *Call It Sleep*. Even more significant is that the kiln of Roth's art was the Lower East Side. Living in Greenwich Village in 1930, Roth was in close proximity to that furnace of ambition and creativity both in terms of years and miles. As an old man living in a mobile home in New Mexico, he may have been too far both geographically and chronologically from the teeming tenements. Thomas Wolfe was probably right when he uttered the words: "You can't go home again."

Masochistically, perhaps, the reader who has invested so many hours in the history of Ira Stigman, as told by the artist as an old man, wishes that the narrative and the old sage's life has not come to an end. One cannot help but relate to the intimate, unvarnished revelations of a quarter century of another person's life without feeling that some things in one's own life remain unfinished, never to achieve closure.

Additional Reading

Roth, Henry. *Call It Sleep*. Reprint, New York: Farrar, Straus and Giroux, 1991.
———. *Mercy of a Rude Stream*. 4 vols. New York: St. Martin's, 1994–98.
Wirth-Nester, Hanna, ed. *New Essays on "Call It Sleep."* New York: Cambridge University Press, 1996.

Harry Roskolenko

1907–1980

A novelist, poet, and travel writer, Harry Roskolenko (he also wrote under several pseudonyms) made his most memorable contributions to twentieth-century American literature with his three autobiographies: *When I Was Last on Cherry Street* (1965), *The Terrorized, 1945–1950* (1968), and *The Time That Was Then: The Lower East Side, 1900–1914, An Intimate Chronicle* (1971).

Roskolenko was born on Cherry Street on the Lower East Side, the thirteenth of fourteen children born to an immigrant Ukrainian Jewish couple. Eight children died of diseases in Ukraine. One of the six American-born children died of disease on the Lower East Side.

Roskolenko's father had been a miller in the Russian Ukraine. Having been drafted into the army of the czar, after twelve years of service he left the army and fled to America via Siberia and Japan. In New York City he worked as a presser in sweatshops and then in a slaughterhouse on First Avenue, on the present site of the United Nations. He brought his wife to New York City, where they started up a new family.

Harry Roskolenko had very little formal education. At nine he was a factory worker. At fourteen he ran away from home, tramped around, and eventually sailed out of the Port of New York on a merchant ship. During the Great Depression he worked on the WPA Federal Writers' Project, and then went back to sea as a second mate in the merchant marine. During World War II he served as an officer on an army transport in the South Pacific. Roskolenko married Diana Chang in 1948. They had one child and were divorced in 1955.

From the 1950s onward Roskolenko made his living exclusively by writing—not an easy thing to do at any time. He wrote three novels: *Black Is a Man* (1954), *The Mistress* (1954), and *Lan-Lan* (1962). *Black Is a Man* is an allegorical novel about race relations before the African American revolution of the 1960s. A fifty-year-old racist white man, James Oggen, suddenly becomes a black man, a quirk of pigmentation. Life becomes totally threatening for him in a Kafkaesque world. He loses his wife, his friends, and his job. His minister is unable to help him.

Oggen wanders alone through the city as he tries to learn the ways of the "Negro." Sally, a white married neighbor, is sexually aroused by Oggen and sees him as forbidden fruit. She subsequently accuses him of rape. He is arrested and put on trial for his life. Oggen's wife finally comes to his rescue and convinces judge and jury that this black man is her husband and that he has been framed. The novel is a not very believable allegorical indictment of the ridiculousness and cruelty of judging people by the color of their skin.

The Mistress is a bodice-ripping potboiler. Anne Browning, a twenty-five-year-old Park Avenue courtesan graduate of Smith College, wishes to write but also wants a husband. She leaves her lover and sails for France with the money from a legacy that conveniently comes through. On board the ocean liner she becomes acquainted with Stanley, a college-instructor friend of her former lover, who has desired her for a long time.

Stanley pursues Anne around France as she continually refuses to sleep with him. She innocently gets into many scrapes, including becoming mixed up with fascists. Stanley saves her, proposes, and she accepts with the proviso that he let her write a novel before they have children. Roskolenko published *The Mistress* under the pseudonym Colin Ross, clearly implying he was not proud of the final product.

Lan-Lan is Roskolenko's most accomplished novel. It is a tender love story full of the atmosphere of French Indochina and Paris in the 1920s. Dr. Paul Galonon, a Parisian, is a man of conscience and compassion. He leaves the artist and model Genevieve, who is also his lover, to join the colonial administration in Cambodia in order to help fight cholera.

The novel offers a fine description of decadent white colonial life.

Galonon is in conflict with the immoral behavior of his fellow countrymen. One day he meets Lan-Lan, a well-educated Cambodian
nurse. They fall in love and have a little girl. When his tour is up, he
returns to Paris. He intends to bring Lan-Lan and their daughter,
Nakry, to Paris but hesitates because of racial qualms. He wonders if
they will they be happy there, and if the mixed-blood child will fit
in. Surprisingly, Genevieve has waited for him all this time, but after
much soul-searching he chooses his Cambodian family. The Galo-
nons will make their life in Paris for better or for worse.

Following Dienbienphu, the Tet Offensive, the retreat from Sai-
gon, and the Pol Pot genocide, the novel gained a dimension and a
special poignancy Roskolenko never intended. Despite Roskolenko's
liberal politics, his "Orientalism" is condescending. Dr. Galonon
never seriously contemplates a real family existence in Cambodia.
The family must live in the "civilized" West, not the "primitive" East,
where, possibly, it would face less racism.

When I Was Last on Cherry Street is a moving account of a Lower
East Side childhood, a wanderer's youth, the development of a radical, and the sexual life of a passionate, sometimes violent man. Roskolenko's childhood and adolescence on the Lower East Side was a
war scene. He fought as a gang member against the brutally anti-
Semitic Irish youth gangs. He stole, was caught, and was often
beaten. He fought with his father, who sometimes beat him too. He
witnessed his mother being run over by an ice truck, as a result of
which she lost her right arm. A sister was also struck down by a truck
and killed. He ran away from home after a beating by his father and
became a hobo.

Roskolenko's colorful prose and narrative skill make *When Last I
Was on Cherry Street* a powerful read. We see his early stint on a coal
barge on Lake Ontario and later on merchant ships sailing to Mexico and then on to Europe; his days as a Trotskyite Communist Party
member in New York City, where he experiences Stalinist brutality
and terror; and his World War II service as an officer on army trans-
ports in the South Pacific. In the end Roskolenko returns to the
Lower East Side. However, as a result of the grand schemes of Commissioner Robert Moses and others, much of the neighborhood is in

the process of being torn down for municipal projects such as high-rise public housing. His Cherry Street is no more.

Two themes structure the memoir: the rabid anti-Semitism in pre–World War II American life and Roskolenko's sex life, a mélange of casual affairs, longer but unhappy relationships, and encounters with prostitutes from the age of nine. As a warts-and-all portrait of an intelligent and talented Jewish American man's life in the first half of the twentieth century, *When I Was Last on Cherry Street* is unparalleled.

The Terrorized—the title refers to the suffering peoples the author encounters in Indochina—picks up Roskolenko's life from his World War II service in the South Pacific to his Paris sojourn in the 1960s. When Roskolenko returned to the States after the war and settled his affairs in New York City, he boarded a passenger ship and sailed back to Australia in order to resume a passionate relationship with an Australian woman, only to receive a cablegram from her aboard ship informing him that she had married. He immediately fell gravely ill but recovered. In Australia he joined a military team searching for the bodies of Australian and American airmen and soldiers who had been lost in the mountains and jungles of New Guinea during the war.

From New Guinea he proceeded to Southeast Asia, including French Indochina, where his meddling reminds one of Graham Greene's novel *The Ugly American*. Everywhere there are bordellos to frequent and women to seduce and abandon. One, named Genevieve, became the model for the character of the same name in *Lan-Lan*.

While en route to Europe, a brief stopover in Cairo is punctuated by a long description of a night spent with a couple of bar girls. As was the case in England and then in Paris, Roskolenko continually meets political figures to interview and fellow writers whose names pepper his pages. In *The Terrorized* Rosolenko tries hard to prove that his bohemian wanderings constitute an interesting and meaningful life. The former perhaps, but not the latter.

In *The Time That Was Then* Roskolenko refocuses on his Lower East Side childhood. In this narrative his perspective is more sociological. Roskolenko discusses the rise of socialism among immigrant Jewish workers, pointing out that the typical success story was not one of workers rising up through the ranks thanks to unionization but rather by means of personal entrepreneurship, such as starting a small business like a luncheonette.

Consisting of fifteen essays, in this autobiographical volume Roskolenko variously discusses factory work, the famous Cloakmaker's Strike of 1910 that led to the unionization of the clothing industry, medical treatment, Lower East Side politics, the pleasures of Yiddish theaters and cafés, and the role of neighborhood settlement houses. Roskolenko seldom waxes nostalgic in this memoir. Although written late in life, the image of the Lower East Side that emerges remains sharp and clear. Skillful descriptions of such prominent New York personalities as Abraham Cahan locate them in just the right time and place.

Summing up his life, Harry Roskolenko perceptively concluded that he was born and had grown up in a "country" called the Lower East Side where nonviolent socialists set a moral tone and created a political conscience that influenced a much larger country, namely, the United States. His life was one grand adventure. He seemed always to know this and revel in the fact. The pleasure and pride he felt in his life comes through in his writing, especially when he focuses on his humble origins on the Lower East Side.

Additional Reading

Roskolenko, Harry. *The Time That Was Then: The Lower East Side, 1900–1914, An Intimate Chronicle.* New York: Dial, 1971.
———. *When I Was Last on Cherry Street.* New York: Stein and Day, 1965.

Conclusion

A Group Picture from the Williamsburg Bridge

The Jewish American writers of the Lower East Side—plus a handful of other early Jewish American writers who did not emerge from the well of creativity that was New York City's Jewish ghetto but who were born or grew up in Brooklyn, Harlem, or Chicago—launched the great modern tradition of Jewish American literature. Those other writers, like Irving Fineman, Daniel Fuchs, and Meyer Levin, were themselves influenced by the current of literary naturalism, modernism, and ethnicity that flowed from East Broadway to the New York publishing houses and the general American public. The early Jewish American writers created the audience that eventually welcomed the works of Saul Bellow, Allen Ginsberg, Lillian Hellman, Norman Mailer, Bernard Malamud, Arthur Miller, Cynthia Ozick, Chaim Potok, Philip Roth, and other major writers active during the golden age of Jewish American literature.

The early Jewish American writers were only slightly influenced by such Yiddish masters as Mendele Mocher Sforim, Sholom Aleichem, I. L. Peretz, Sholem Asch, and Joseph Opatoshu. They were more impressed by the Russian romanticism that flowed in with those intellectuals who had studied in the Russian-language schools of Lithuania. Of course, early Jewish American writers read and were influenced by Karl Marx and Friedrich Engels. Most were socialists and a few were communists until they became disillusioned by Stalinism.

The early writers also read the classic nineteenth-century works by such British novelists as Charles Dickens and George Eliot. Most significantly, they assimilated the strict realist and looser impressionist styles, the penchant for description, the subjects, values, and democratic impulses of such contemporary Anglo-American writers as Edward Bellamy, Stephen Crane, Theodore Dreiser, O. Henry, William Dean Howells, Frank Norris, and Upton Sinclair, among others. The new Jewish American writers shared the same social concerns of the "Anglo-Americans": economic insecurity, industrial conflict, the abuse of privilege, and the ravages of competitive capitalism. They embraced reportage and environmental analysis, especially after they read about themselves and their environs in the sociological works of Jacob Riis (a Danish immigrant and early master of the photodocumentary), such as *How the Other Half Lives* (1890), *The Children of the Poor* (1892), *The Battle with the Slum* (1902), and *Children of the Tenements* (1903); as well as Hutchins Hapgood's *Spirit of the Ghetto* (1902).

The first generation of Jewish American writers were much less interested in Henry James, Edith Wharton, and Willa Cather because the milieus depicted by these writers were too alien to the ghetto-dwelling immigrants and their children. But the ubiquitously popular Mark Twain made writing in dialect acceptable.

Photography and painting gave salience to the Lower East Side over other immigrant sites. Even at the height of the Jewish immigration period during the turn of the twentieth century, the area attracted visitors from across America who were "slumming." The members of the Ash Can School of American painters, such as George Bellows, John Sloan, and George Luks, roamed below Fourteenth Street in search of "exotic" faces and places for the consumption of the general American public. One child of immigrants, the sculptor Jacob Epstein, began his artistic career while living on Hester Street and sketching his neighbors for Hapgood's *Spirit of the Ghetto*.

The early Jewish American writers did much of their reading in the two main public libraries available to the Lower East Side, namely, the Astor on Lafayette Street and the Seward on East Broadway. They bought new and used books from the shops on East Broadway, Grand Street, and Essex Street. Even in the 1940s used-book stores abounded on the Lower East Side. Classics by American, British, and continental European writers were sold for nickels and dimes. (I purchased the imperialist adventure stories of the boys' writer G. A. Henty for five or ten cents apiece and dreamed of military exploits and warfare, fighting for the glory of the British Empire in the Punjab or the New Zealand home of the Maori.)

When they still lived on the Lower East Side the Jewish American writers discussed literature in the teahouses, coffee shops, and cafeterias on Second Avenue, East Broadway, and Fourteenth Street. Conversations were heated and loud. Arguments over politics and aesthetics might have led to blows but never did.

Immediacy and authenticity were attributes shared by most first-generation Jewish American writers when documenting Lower East Side life. For the immigrants and their children the fact that one of their own, like Cahan or Yezierska, was writing about their lives empowered them. It made them seem less like a subhuman specimen intended for the sociological microscope or the touristic gaze. The visibility created by their own writers, though unvarnished, offered a dignified human portrait, as opposed to the often vicious caricatures in the popular press.

Thus, the literary texts of the first generation of Jewish American writers were extremely important cultural artifacts linking the immigrant community to the wider world. Furthermore, subsequent generations of American Jews were able, once past a degree of mythification, to see in the trials and struggles of their grandparents and great grandparents a heroic story, an exodus that matched the Zionism of those late-nineteenth- and early-twentieth-century Jews who took the route to Palestine to find freedom. The immigrants, like the Zionists, endured and triumphed in an epic journey that later generations could and would be proud of. In a relatively short time the descendants of the immigrants came to admire all that their forebears had endured and how they had survived and flourished, eventually overcoming considerable hostility in their newly adopted land. They are no longer disparaged as "greenhorns," embarrassingly ignorant simple folk who didn't even speak the language of the land. In the course of writing this book, I have come to realize just how remarkable were the life journeys of my grandparents and parents—although they never thought so. Significantly, the depiction of the courage, suffering, obstacles, and achievements of the Eastern European Jews in

America also served to ameliorate the anger and assuage the shame some American Jews felt with respect to the seeming passivity of the many European Jews who staggered without protest to the German death camps.

In the great American tradition of "Westward Ho!" the early Lower East Side Jewish American writers portrayed their parents and themselves as proud American pioneers whose frontiers were the visible and invisible walls of a great metropolis; whose enemies, to be vanquished through reason and not by force, were the legions of anti-Semites; and whose goal was complete acceptance as a valued part of the American social fabric. They hoped to achieve some sort of integration without completely sacrificing their Jewish identity. The quest continues.

The literature of the first generation of Jewish American authors could not have been produced in any place in America but the Lower East Side. Nor could it have appeared at any other time. The novels, stories, and poems are both a reflection of and an integral part of their context. The legacy of the early Jewish American writers includes: the pain of adjustment; guilt at abandoning the European past and the customs of the Old World; and criticism of the ruthless, capitalist bent in American life while simultaneously striving to obtain and enjoy the freedoms and material opportunities it offered them.

The work of the early Jewish American writers is, for the most part, devoid of Jewish self-hatred—a reaction to marginalization that attempts to identify with the majority by buying into the majority's negative stereotypes of Jews. In service to the Jewish community, either consciously or unconsciously, the writers struggled to maintain some semblance of Old World Jewish cultural identity while assimilating within the ubiquitous American culture. In the process, the Lower East Siders abandoned the Yiddish language of their parents. English was the literary language of the future. They were desperate to become fluent in it, to access the literary riches of their new culture. As poets, playwrights, and writers of fiction, they strove to reach the vast American audience, which they succeeded in doing. American literature has made room for ethnic writers from their time to the present.

Finally, the early Jewish American writers also influenced American literature. Thanks to courageous New York City publishers, they brought a true image of the Jewish immigrant into the mainstream of American literature. They made possible the accurate portrayal of later immigrant groups and, indeed, even such earlier immigrant groups as the Famine Irish. Preferring autobiographical fiction, these authors made subjects of themselves and their families. The source of this subjectivity may have been European high modernism, but the early Jewish American writers helped legitimize the technique in American fiction.

Writers are notoriously hard on their families as well as on themselves. It is the price of authenticity. From the beginning Jewish American writers have known this. At their best they have avoided the dangers of sentimentality, idealization, and romanticized nostalgia. The influence of the early Jewish American writers on the second and third generation of Jewish authors and those to come is inestimable and unending.

Selected Bibliography

Index

Selected Bibliography

Diner, Hasia R. *Lower East Side Memories: A Jewish Place in America*. Princeton, N.J.: Princeton University Press, 2000.

———, Jeffrey Shandler, and Beth S. Wenger, eds. *Remembering the Lower East Side: American Jewish Reflections*. Bloomington: Indiana University Press, 2000.

Ewen, Elizabeth. *Immigrant Women in the Land of Dollars: Life and Culture on the Lower East Side, 1890–1925*. New York: Monthly Review Press, 1985.

Freeman, Jonathan. *The Temple of Culture: Assimilation and Anti-Semitism in Literary America*. New York: Oxford University Press, 1999.

Friedman-Kasaba, Kathie. *Memories of Migration: Gender, Ethnicity, and Work in the Lives of Jewish and Italian Women in New York, 1870–1924*. Albany: State University of New York Press, 1996.

Hapgood, Hutchins. *The Spirit of the Ghetto*. New York: Funk & Wagnalls, 1902. Reprint, Cambridge, Mass.: Belknap Press, Harvard University Press, 1967.

———. *Types from City Streets*. New York: Funk & Wagnalls, 1910. Reprint, New York: Garrett, 1970.

Highman, John. *Send These to Me: Jews and Other Immigrants in Urban America*. New York: Atheneum, 1975. Revised ed., Baltimore: Johns Hopkins University Press, 1984.

Hindus, Milton, ed. *The Jewish East Side, 1881–1924*. New Brunswick, N.J.: Transaction, 1996.

Howe, Irving. *World of Our Fathers*. New York: Harcourt, Brace, 1976.

———, and Kenneth Libo. *A Documentary History of Immigrant Jews in America, 1880–1930*. New York: Richard Marek, 1979.

Israelowitz, Oscar. *Lower East Side Tourbook*. Brooklyn, N.Y.: Israelowitz Publishing, 1996.

Lifson, David S. *The Yiddish Theatre in America*. New York: Thomas Yoseloff, 1965.

Maffi. Mario. *Gateway to the Promised Land: Ethnic Cultures in New York's Lower East Side*. New York: New York University Press. 1995.

Moore, Deborah Dash. *At Home in America: Second Generation New York Jews*. New York: Columbia University Press, 1981.

Pinsker, Sanford. *Jewish-American Fiction, 1917–1987*. New York: Twayne, 1992.

Rischen, Moses. *The Promised City: New York's Jews, 1870–1914*. Cambridge, Mass.: Harvard University Press, 1962. Reprint, 1977.

Bibliography

Rubin, Rachel. *Jewish Gangsters of Modern Literature.* Urbana: University of Illinois Press, 2000.

Sanders, Ronald. *The Downtown Jews: Portrait of an Immigrant Generation.* New York: Harper and Row, 1969.

Sandrow, Nahma. *Vagabond Stars: A World History of Yiddish Theater.* New York: Harper and Row, 1977. Reprint, Syracuse, N.Y.: Syracuse University Press, 1995.

Schoener, Allon, ed. *Portal to America: The Lower East Side, 1870–1925.* New York: Holt, Rinehart, and Winston, 1967.

Shatzky, Joel, and Michael Taub, eds. *Contemporary Jewish-American Writers: A Bio-Critical Sourcebook.* Westport, Conn.: Greenwood Press, 1997.

Weinberg, Sydney Stahl. *The World of Our Mothers: The Lives of Jewish Immigrant Women.* New York: Shocken, 1988.

Index

Index